There was truth and there was untruth
and if you clung to the truth
even against the whole world,
you were not mad.

GEORGE ORWELL

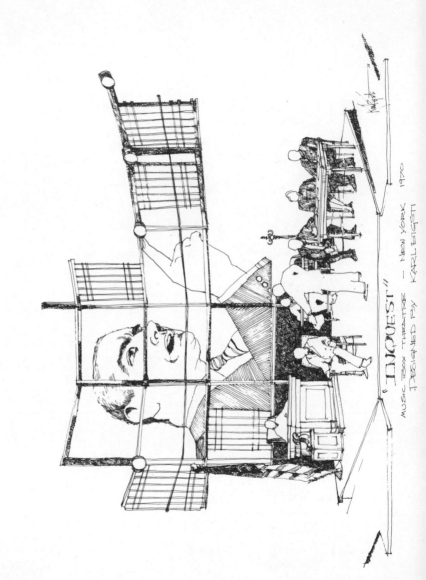

"INQUEST"

MUSIC BOX THEATRE — NEW YORK 1970
DESIGNED BY KARL EIGSTI

Inquest

A Play by Donald Freed

Based, in part, on Invitation to an Inquest *by Walter and Miriam Schneir and* The Judgment of Julius and Ethel Rosenberg *by John Wexley*

A SPOTLIGHT DRAMABOOK

Hill and Wang New York

For the Sobells

Contents

Inquest

The Case and the Myth: *The United States of America v. Julius and Ethel Rosenberg*

The Case

The Case—what the Government always called "the atom spy ring"—was my political baptism. Whether it was—as Jean-Paul Sartre called it—the start of World War III or not, it certainly was the start for many of us in the fifties of what was to become known in the sixties as "the movement." But in those days the headlines handed down the fateful news of doomsday. It was as if the atom, like Zeus's fire, had been stolen from Heaven, while the Rosenbergs and Morton Sobell played the roles of anti-heroes. It was the Government that dominated the stage with its federal agents, lawyers, judges, Congressmen, and armies of functionaries. It was the United States v. the USSR and the "spies" were only attendant lords in the cosmic drama. We in the public received our mythology from the front pages, and thousands of people who were later—through dint of hard study of transcripts and evidence—to become either expert in or obsessed with The Case followed from day to day the cartoon-like melodrama of the editorial imagination. At first we all thought them guilty.

What first made some of us suspicious? It was not the "old left" of the day that first cracked my own particular mythology of virtue and patriotism. It was the well-known legal experts who first fascinated me. So they—the "spies"—were all dead or imprisoned before I began to say: "Wait!"

1

As the years went by I became both expert and obsessed. The dim figures of The Case began to take on definition. The Rosenbergs began to be real and so, too, did the Government. Roy Cohn and Joseph McCarthy were the agents of the Government and the authors of its new religion: anti-communism. Something was rotten. The Cold War froze to zero degree. Books, opinions, journals, authorities from all over the world, were beginning to be univocal about the conduct of the judge, about the plague-like atmosphere of what was already being called (somewhat unfairly) the "McCarthy Era," about The Case in general. Now The Case was becoming The Scandal.

But there were two reasons why there could be no play then. First, there was the frozen, frightened political climate, and second, in my opinion, there was no coherent aesthetic vocabulary yet available.

The Future Determines the Past

"The future determines the past," Morton Sobell said one night after he was released. After a generation behind bars for "conspiracy to commit espionage." That is, the past becomes received myth unless or until artists and critics begin a revision or de-mythologization. In a time when the very breathing is poisoned by the ideas of the past it is a part of the burden of the writer, through fact and cruelty, to help in the construction of these new anti-myths—whether plays or films or books—that are meant to be a revelation and a therapy.

The anti-myth must have a reflexive structure; it is the double of the myth that it is confronting. There are the gods—the gods of the twentieth century—Freud, Marx, Nietzsche, and the chorus is none other than the terrible Man in the Street; the oracle is the media; the song and dance is that of the couch and the court and the street and the barricade. And there is no beginning or middle or end in sight.

2

Liberals, Radicals and Revolutionaries

For the "liberal," the meaning of a case like *The United States of America v. Julius and Ethel Rosenberg, et al.* does not turn on guilt or innocence, but only on the astounding and unprecedented death penalty exacted by a panic-stricken and twitching majority. The "radical" is obsessed with the innocence of the victims and his is a rage to tell the truth even if the earth opens at his feet. The "revolutionary" assumes the inequity of the trial with the liberal, shares an identification with the victim as does the radical, but for him the innocence of the victim is less weighty than the *guilt of the State*. And he goes for the Government. He demands of the State a quick accounting. The new historians (the "revisionists") and some of the new playwrights of Fact and Cruelty are attempting this. Once man against Fate, now everyman v. the State.

This is existential work, for the public past of America is gone and dead as the Rosenbergs. If it were not gone, then we could change it. We, none of us, can change the past (that is the fact and the cruelty), but we can, if we are sufficiently lucid, *determine* it, given the weight of information that the play intends. These new anti-myths do not invoke terror and pity in the old way, rather they try for something like anguish and, perhaps, a radical solidarity.

From Kaufman to Hoffman

From Irving Kaufman, of the great atom spy trials, to Julius Hoffman, of the trial of the conspiracy of youth and peace and black liberation, it is only a fraction of a second in political time. Jerry Rubin and Bobby Seale are the epigonoi of Morton Sobell as surely as the struggle has moved from the courts into the streets and back to the courts again. That passage is the passage of time. The charge, "conspiracy," is the same; the State's tactics are stereotyped; silence in the face of power is the same now as then. But the critical difference is in the reactions of people.

3

The Case and the Myth

Where once there was guilt and paralysis, now there is rebellion and movement. Once a handful of men and committees could cow millions of people into silence, now the Army has been in the streets and yet the pressure for change goes up by the numbers.

Here is the vocabulary of the myth of the twentieth century: film, tape, trials, technology, confessions—in short, the State and its visible paraphernalia. The infrastructure of the myth is the agony and confrontation between Science and Magic. The Rosenbergs and Morton Sobell were players in this myth. The anti-myth to the magic of the State is Theatre of Fact. The anti-myth to the science of the State is Theatre of Cruelty.

The goal of the anti-myth is not guilt but another feeling entirely—the one Marx called revolutionary—*shame.*

Guilt is pervasive and equals repetition; shame is specific, rooted in fact and leads to change. Shame is the recognition of choices past and present. Shame posits the reality of *freedom* and thus choice. Shame has as its components elements of fact and cruelty. Shame is the precondition for hope in modern man.

Theatre of Cruelty

The two new theatres of Fact and Cruelty provide a grammar, at last, for a popular drama of the twentieth century. All exponential numbers, facts and figures, names and dates and places are necessary to even begin to come close to the phenomena of our time: the death camps, the great purge trials, the Triple Revolution and most of all the atom bomb. But for the interpretation of all these facts it also requires cruelty. The spectator must be given a choice in order to retain any hope that he can influence the monstrosities that lie before him.

The popular idea of this new theatre as a grotesque circus holds for *Inquest.* There is the "Man in the Street" chorus. These are the masses ruined, as Tolstoy diagnosed, by the "Government." The folk who twitch to the signals and magic of science like so many Kafkaesque or Dostoyevskian pale criminals.

4

Next, there are the "creatures of the State," as Whittaker Chambers called them. The professional prosecution witnesses condemned to talk and point forever—poor mad monsters (Harry Gold babbled endlessly of black snakes and secret agents; David Greenglass could never stop smiling). Finally, there are the gods of the twentieth century—Marx, Freud, Nietzsche—under whose prophetic gaze the doomsday scenario must be acted out to the end.

The Theatre of Cruelty is surreal in one sense, but this is balanced out against the torment of choice and freedom inherent in the will to survive the nightmare. To wake up is, in itself, an act of hope.

For the New York production of this play, Ken Isaacs prepared a series of aural-visual souvenirs ("The Bomb," "The Spy Ring"). The sights and sounds of the Cold War past, from Milton Berle to Joseph McCarthy, can take the audience back in time, jog their memories and make them recall that it all happened. This is what I mean as one kind of Theatre of Cruelty: to be made to remember and therefore to want to choose and change the past, but to be unable to because the past no longer exists, and because the past no longer exists (and that is why we feel such pain), to know that we are free.

Theatre of Fact

The transcripts and memoranda and tapes are there. Every word no matter how bizarre or poisoned can be documented. It all happened. But I do not think the Theatre of Fact can stand alone. I believe that the increments must be thrown into a cruel relief and that reconstructions can and should be drawn from them. When we see Ethel and Julius Rosenberg in love, or Ethel talking to her psychoanalyst, or the two of them talking in prison, we have no choice but to reconstruct from the primary sources of letters and conversations, and memories again.

Predictably, there is loud and quick complaint that the "facts" are merely out-of-context abstractions that can be manipulated

5

to prove anything. "Commitment" is branded as rank bias and propaganda. It is true that the technology of film and tape behind this new theatre can be perverted—we know that about any technology—but media, when it is authentic, can also explode the myths of the status quo and make rending gaps in the credibility of the "establishment" of lies.

"Without continual freedom of choice, there can be no dramatic conflict." The assertion by Rolf Hochhuth is now and will be in the future the libido of the new theatre.

It is for the dramatist to infiltrate the huge historical abstractions of the time and to bring out from the flux recognizable human beings and a confluence of "all too human" motives to sweep us along to the rational and non-rational understandings of otherwise unspeakable events.

When events are so momentous as to be unspeakable, only myth (poetry) or statistics will begin to encompass and abstract what would otherwise be lost to understandings. It is this planned alienation that makes for the aesthetics, or part of them, of the Theatre of Fact. But the impact of the Theatre of Fact is not purgative like the Theatre of Cruelty: the latter is therapeutic, the former didactic.

How to distinguish the Theatre of Fact from such earlier twentieth-century genres as Social Realism, Naturalism, and the Living Newspaper? The Theatre of Social Realism was a revolutionary and anti-romantic attempt to imitate life in a new way. It was a celebration of late nineteenth-century myth, the myth of mass man in everyday life, and the smallest detail would register with a new impact on those who had been "poisoned by romanticism." The plays of Hauptmann, Gorki, Ibsen, the others, took us through the fourth wall into the microcosm of a Berlin or New York street, a Russian country estate, or a Scandinavian bourgeoisie, into the infrastructure of daily life. All this was dubbed Naturalism and that, in any case, was the aim. How shocked the new century was by this analysis of the selected fateful trivia of the everyday—Zola and Freud, chemistry and psychology—how true it all was!

6

But the Theatre of Fact deals not with the banal or quotidian smudges of life. Rather it has to do with the colossal, the overarching new myth of Evil: the titanic symbol of the camps; the assassination of a leader; murder while "good people" look on; mighty nation-states pitted against small scapegoats; 100,000 victims in the first second. This content, then, is, so far, quite different—and its structure is even more so. These plays most closely resemble "histories," in the old terminology, that have begun to bleed through into the media of the man in the street.

The Play

The story of The United States of America v. Julius and Ethel Rosenberg, et al. is Theatre of Fact in that every word is taken from primary sources. At its most lunatic there is not an invented word in the entire text. The reconstructions ("Love," "Money," "Dreams") are drawn from letters, notes, always memory. But the mise-en-scène of the play is Theatre of Cruelty. Stage A is the court; Stage B is the psyche and history. There is an incessant dialectic.

We are combining not only media but also the facts of evil with the cruelty of individual choice. What you see really happened; that is fact. Now you must let it happen to you; that is existential or moral cruelty: You who were passive and did not choose when you had the chance must now undergo everything twice, only now it is forbidden you, that choice, by finitude and time.

The new theatre is like the old in its drive to penetrate into the springs of existence. The shock of the numbers and images, in a play like Inquest, is meant to be therapeutic, for it is as George Orwell said: "There was truth and there was untruth and if you clung to the truth even against the whole world, you were not mad."

These two new forms of drama, which build out of the past, deal with man no longer as if he were made in the image of a machine but as a desperately ill, thousand-year-old mad animal.

7

But a human animal, however ravaged, is not a machine, and there can be hope for recovery. Here the old cathartic function of the performing arts is invoked again, and the aim of the theatre of the future in this century may very well be, in the words Weiss gives Marat, to remind the suffering that—

> The important thing
> is to pull yourself up by your own
>   hair
> to turn yourself inside out
> and see the whole world with fresh
>   eyes

Soon it will require courage, once again, to go to the theatre as the twentieth century begins—fatefully—to purge itself. Cruelty is its abreaction, and Fact its therapy.

Disenthrallment

"We must disenthrall ourselves," said Lincoln when the crisis deepened. That is what these theatres of Fact and Cruelty are about. For many, the American Dream has simply become the American Nightmare, but that, too, is, I think, transitory.

In the twentieth century we have begun to frighten ourselves to death with grotesque and mindless abstractions: "the Government," "the masses," "the power structure," "the outsider." These are our myths and—like the ancients—we really believe them. The difference is that their myths were theirs and served them, whereas ours are invented and received and have made us sick. Racial and political myths can best be subverted, perhaps, by those who should know the most about storytelling—the playwrights. So the play is an anti-myth; it means to disenthrall.

What, then, shall be the new myths? That is for the real and new people to create; the playwrights will come later. They will write under the sign of Artaud, who, more than McLuhan, is the genius behind the new "Theatre of Time" that is coming:

We are not free and the sky can still fall on our heads and the theatre exists to remind us of that first of all. For now the theatres of Fact and Cruelty are theatres of absurd hope. Just now we are all involved, alike, in making the necessary "myth of the twenty-first century." Oh, gods, grant us credibility.

DONALD FREED

April 23, 1970
New York City

Inquest

Dramatis Personae

EMANUEL BLOCH: A kindly, and in this case fatally gentle, defense lawyer. He spent the last years of his life in futile attempts to have the death sentence of the Rosenbergs commuted.

ROY COHN: At the time of the trial, a young man in his twenties. His great success in the prosecution of the Rosenbergs led on to his notorious career as counsel and colleague of Senator Joseph R. McCarthy. Recent years have blackened his name and he has become a symbol of the crisis of confidence in the Government that developed in America in the 1950's.

HARRY GOLD: A bizarre character called onto the stage of history by the times in which we live. A nonentity whose fantasies tallied with those in power.

DAVID GREENGLASS: The always smiling younger brother of Ethel Rosenberg and, with his wife, Ruth, the only witness against her. His wife was never indicted and he served only ten years, though they both confessed to the same crime for which the Rosenbergs received the death penalty.

RUTH GREENGLASS: David Greenglass' wife. Poor, fierce, and cunning. The Government depended on her to keep her husband in line and credible. She "confessed" but was not even indicted.

TESSIE GREENGLASS: *Ethel Rosenberg's mother. An illiterate, embittered woman, hostile to her daughter and everyone else except her son David and his wife.*

IRVING KAUFMAN: *The "boy judge" who led his law class at Fordham University and became, because of his espionage trials in the 1950's, a famous federal judge.*

ETHEL ROSENBERG: *From the same deprived environment as the Greenglasses, Ethel Rosenberg was, nevertheless, a socially and aesthetically developed woman. Her life was ordinary in every way until her brother's petty thieving and psychopathic personality selected her to play an incredible role whose first avatar ended in the electric chair at Ossining Prison on June 19, 1953.*

JULIUS ROSENBERG: *He was three years younger than his wife and a man of the Depression. Idealistic and a failure in his one business attempt. He became known as the mastermind of Soviet espionage and the perpetrator of the "crime of the century." He died six minutes before his wife with what The New York Times called "amazing calm."*

IRVING SAYPOL: *The senior attorney for the Government in the great espionage cases of the fifties. He was subsequently made a judge.*

ANN SIDOROVICH: *She refused to be intimidated. There were many.*

THE COMPANY and the MAN IN THE STREET

Throughout, Judge Kaufman appears as THE COURT, *Saypol and Cohn appear as* THE GOVERNMENT, *and Emanuel Bloch appears as* THE DEFENSE.

Inquest opened in New York at The Music Box theatre on April 23, 1970, in a shortened, one-act version directed by Alan Schneider. Special projections were by Ken Isaacs; settings by Karl Eigsti; costumes by Sara Brook; lighting by Jules Fisher; sound by Gary Harris. The cast was as follows:

ETHEL ROSENBERG   Anne Jackson
JULIUS ROSENBERG   George Grizzard
EMANUEL BLOCH   James Whitmore
CLERK   Allen Garfield
BAILIFF   Abe Vigoda
IRVING SAYPOL   Mason Adams
ROY COHN   Mike Bursten
JUDGE KAUFMAN   Michael Lipton
REPORTER   Charles Kindl
REPORTER   David Clarke
DAVID GREENGLASS   Jack Hollander
FBI AGENTS   Ed Bordo, Abe Vigoda, David Clarke
TESSIE GREENGLASS   Sylvie Straus
MATRON   Sylvia Gassell
HARRY GOLD   Phil Leeds
RABBI   Allen Garfield
RUTH GREENGLASS   Hildy Brooks

Chronology of Events

1945

August 6   Hiroshima atom bombed. Dead: 80,000 in the first minute.

August 9   Nagasaki: 75,000 dead.

1949

September 23   Announcement of Russian atom bomb explosion.

1950

February 3   Dr. Klaus Fuchs confesses to atomic espionage for Soviet Union.

May 23   Harry Gold confesses to being Fuchs's American link in spy ring.

June 15   David Greenglass arrested as Gold's accomplice.

June 25   Korean War begins.

July 17   Julius Rosenberg arrested as co-conspirator with Gold and Greenglass.

August 11   Ethel Rosenberg arrested on the same charges as her husband, Julius.

August 18   Morton Sobell arrested as co-conspirator.

1951

March 6   Rosenberg-Sobell spy ring trial begins.

April 5   Julius and Ethel Rosenberg sentenced to death. Morton Sobell sentenced to thirty years.

1953

February 11   President Eisenhower denies clemency.

June 19   Many courts and appeals later (the record of the trial was never reviewed by the Supreme Court), Julius and Ethel Rosenberg are executed at 8:02 P.M. and 8:08 P.M., respectively.

1969

January 14   Morton Sobell is paroled.

Design for the Sidewalk and Lobby

The experience starts on the street with projectors mounted overhead (under marquee) which throw images down to the sidewalk. Exterior lighting must be muted and sidewalk may have to be painted light gray to receive the images.

These are chosen from the large head shots, demonstration (massive textures of people) shots, maps and the two A-bomb sketches made by Greenglass. The strong central images register well and serve to familiarize the audience with the persons in the play—after seating, the familiarity cuts the distance between actors and audience.

The lobby area is largely a print media area with newspaper pages blown up to six-foot vertical dimension and mounted on wall panels and doors. The pages bear headlines which appear later in the play. The contextual material from the papers will be strong here . . . creating the atmospheres and vibrations of the fifties.

The right and left walls (as you enter) to be covered with large panels of the gods (Freud, Nietzsche, and Marx)—large head shots six feet high rendered in high contrast photography (i.e., the grays are all dropped out and only the black and white portions of the pictures remain to make images like branding irons).

The gods' images will bear their names in cool Helvetica type face and the whole assembly is the dialectic between the cool,

17

considered mien of the gods and the incredibly momentary statement-structure of the news media. Contemplation, thought, and deep feeling in collision with franticness.

Speakers and tape in the lobby will deliver an audio track composed of sound fragments of the fifties. McCarthy, Eisenhower, Truman, Dewey, Fibber and Molly, Berle, Lucy, laugh tracks—a sound collage that time-machines you back into those years.

If there is enough lobby room there should be a great primary structure hanging from the ceiling. This structure will be designed and patterned to translate the time-continuum of the whole Rosenberg event so the audience can place themselves with relation to the action and also get a fix on three or four salient features of the action. This may keep them from getting lost later.

The time-armature (above) will also provide (when seen overall, in unity) a basic translation of the case without detail. This overview is important.

KEN ISAACS

April, 1970
New York City

Prologue

The Dialectic

Full screen of Supreme Court yearly pictures with entire area blue-gelled except for circle surrounding the head of JUSTICE FELIX FRANKFURTER.

Albert Einstein stamp (8¢) repeated en bloc over whole screen authenticates with "United States" as his statement runs.

THE VOICE OF FRANKFURTER   To be writing an opinion in a case affecting two lives after the curtain has been rung down upon them has the appearance of pathetic futility. But history also has its claims.

THE VOICE OF EINSTEIN   From the viewpoint of restoring sanity to our political climate, one must not let this case rest.

The Bomb

Einstein remains on one screen.

Building up around him are the images of the early times of the atom from Los Alamos. Trinity Project ground plan, early atomic pile photos, $E = MC^2$ appears on several screens. Mushroom clouds, Oppenheimer at tower, Fermi, Los Alamos Newsletter sheets, Fat Man and Big Boy (Hiroshima and Nagasaki).

Switch from Einstein stamp to real shot of him in above process.

Bomb remains in center screen, then changes to red circle—small.

19

Combat shot of B-29 bomber appears on one upper screen above red circle.

Lower line of screens has complete horizontal coverage with Hiroshige prints of places, people, and things in color. Includes samurai and full-figure lady dressing.

Plane moves off to right, bomb (red spot) enlarges over field, and prints are replaced by frieze of Japanese pedestrians along bottom of screen.

Note that open slides in above events are blue for sky translation.

Red disc as the bomb enlarges and the pedestrian frieze goes into very high contrast (like the burned-in shadow on the wall of the building in Hiroshima).

Shift to a full heroic screen picture of smiling Japanese children —a texture of nine or ten happy young heads with red and orange gel over (the fire).

At this point different but intense gels in red and orange alternate over screens and images.

Zoom back from the kids as they move away from us at awesome speed (by going from full-screen to one unit). As they move back and become small, they are also displaced from one screen to another in the central area, popping back.

After the kids reach the last position, a heavy black diagonal X covers them.

The gel fire storm rages as slides of the pulverization and rubble texture that is Hiroshima build up on the screen. Contorted faces, mountains of rubble, headlines in ten languages, siren, screams, moans. The climax is the sobbing of one child.

Sound for this event should be men talking (but indistinctly), machinery and metal-to-metal clinks, typewriters, generator whines, and a mannerly boom for the experiment in the desert, plus Geiger counters (this all for Los Alamos).

20

Noise of four engines of plane blunt cut with countryside bird noises for delivery sequence followed by noises of wind and bomb. Pure electronic sound with structured frequency and volume.

At the zenith the fire storm races across the screen. Silence. Then we hear and see, in the darkness, the gods of the twentieth century—Marx, Freud, Nietzsche—appear and disappear. The "red alert" wail, the atomic "music," rises and falls behind the oracles. The gods appear hypnotically. The MAN IN THE STREET, *like survivors of an atom bombing, speaks.*

MAN IN THE STREET   Nietzsche, have mercy on us.

THE VOICE OF NIETZSCHE   We live in a period of atoms and atomic chaos, and that terrible apparition—the Nation-State.

MAN IN THE STREET   Freud, have mercy on us.

THE VOICE OF FREUD   Men have brought their powers of subduing the forces of nature to such a pitch that by using them they could now very easily exterminate one another to the last man. They know this—hence arises their current unrest, their dejection, their mood of apprehension.

MAN IN THE STREET   Marx, have mercy on us.

THE VOICE OF MARX   If we set out to discover the impelling forces which stand behind historical figures, and constitute the true final impulses of history, we cannot consider so much the motive of single individuals, as those which set in motion great masses and entire nations.

In slow motion, the atom bomb media resume. Through the flames the time chamber of the 1950's begins to bleed into visibility. First comes the popular cultural axis: early television laugh tracks vie with the cries of the bomb victims; a song like "Cry" canceling the sirens; sports heroes; the big mouths of expensive cars and Milton Berle and Walter Winchell, etc. Next comes the political axis: the brutal comedy routine shares space with Joseph McCarthy; the political imagery of the American Cold War is established before the last layer of media—the "Atom Spy Ring" case itself—is firmly imprinted. A dating process is evolved from the rash of headlines.

The fall-out of sights and sounds slows and drops until only frozen images remain on the various screens.

THE SCREEN

EVERY WORD YOU WILL HEAR OR SEE ON THIS STAGE IS A DOCUMENTED QUOTATION FROM TRIAL TRANSCRIPTS AND ORIGINAL SOURCES OR A RECONSTRUCTION FROM ACTUAL EVENTS.

Picture of J. EDGAR HOOVER.

THE VOICE OF J. EDGAR HOOVER   The twentieth century has witnessed the intrusion into its body fabric of a highly malignant cancer—a cancer which threatens to destroy Judaic-Christian civilization. In the final analysis the Communist worldview must be met and defeated by the Christian worldview.

Picture of RICHARD NIXON.

THE VOICE OF RICHARD NIXON   If the President says the American people are entitled to know all the facts, I feel the American people are entitled to know the facts about the espionage ring which was responsible for turning over information on the atom bomb to the agents of the Russian government.

The Spy Ring

The head of KLAUS FUCHS *covers the screen. Headlines tell the story of his arrest. On one screen the diagram of the Spy Ring begins. This is a cancer-like network. The "Communist Cancer," of the Hoover worldview, is in the paranoid style.*

THE VOICE OF KLAUS FUCHS   There are other crimes which I have committed other than the ones with which I'm charged. When I asked my counsel to put certain facts before you, I did so in order to atone for *these* crimes. They are not crimes in the eyes of the law.

THE VOICE OF J. EDGAR HOOVER Communist man is a brute, ideologically trained . . . he is immune to the emotions of pity, sorrow or remorse. He is truly an alarming monster, human in physical form, but in practice a cynically godless and immoral machine.

THE VOICE OF RICHARD NIXON We found that in the last seven years six hundred million people had been lost to the Communists and not a single Russian soldier had been lost in combat. The Communists are nibbling us to death in little wars all over the world.

Picture of JOSEPH MCCARTHY.

THE VOICE OF JOSEPH MCCARTHY I have here in my hand a list of two hundred and five that were known to the Secretary of State as being members of the Communist Party.

THE VOICE OF J. EDGAR HOOVER The secret of the atomic bomb has been stolen. *Find the thieves!*

Film of HARRY GOLD *being taken into custody. Headlines give information. The diagram of the "Ring" expands, including* GOLD's *head.*

THE SCREEN
PHILADELPHIA CHEMIST, HARRY GOLD, NAMED BY THE FBI, AS KLAUS FUCH'S AMERICAN CONTACT IN RUSSIAN SPY RING

THE VOICE OF J. EDGAR HOOVER In all the history of the FBI, there never was a more important problem than this one, never another case where we felt under such pressure. The unknown man simply had to be found.

Film of DAVID GREENGLASS *being taken into custody. Headlines and the diagram of the Ring tell the story.*

23

Film of JULIUS *and* ETHEL ROSENBERG *being arrested. Headlines for the arrest of the* ROSENBERGS *appear on the screen.*

THE SCREEN

NEW YORKER SEIZED AS ATOM SPY
GOT LOS ALAMOS ATOM BOMB DATA
FOR SOVIET RING

PLOT TO HAVE GI GIVE BOMB DATA
TO SOVIET IS LAID TO HIS SISTER

On opposite corners, in tight spotlight, stand JULIUS *and* ETHEL ROSENBERG.

ETHEL ROSENBERG . . . after a listless game of handball (played solo, of course), a shower, dinner and an evening of enchanting music, during which you made passionate love to me, I . . . finally succumbed to homesick tears. . . . Oh, darling, how greedy I am for life and living.

JULIUS ROSENBERG At this moment I'm very lethargic and in a romantic mood. I guess it is the combined effect of a nice long spring day and a natural desire to be with my beloved. . . . Everything seems so unreal and out of focus. . . . It seems like we're suspended somewhere far off, seeing everything that's being done and not being able to do anything even though we are the center of controversy.

On the screen headlines give information. The diagram of the "Ring" expands, including GOLD'S, GREENGLASS', *and the* ROSENBERGS' *heads.*

THE VOICE OF J. EDGAR HOOVER The unknown man simply had to be found!

EMANUEL BLOCH *appears in a pool of light on the quiet stage.*

EMANUEL BLOCH In the middle of dinner, the phone rang: a man I had never met named Julius Rosenberg asked if I could see him. We took a little walk, it was a nice night, and I said to him, "Mr. Rosenberg, I don't think you have anything to worry about." I figured it was probably something minor, like a loyalty oath case. So, I was the defense.

He shakes his head and sighs.

I had no idea of what was waiting for me. They were arrested in July and August of 1950 and executed in June of 1953—in between was the trial. That's all I know.

Pause.

I was the defense but I can't tell you what really happened to those two human beings. Let me put it to you this way—the future determines the past.

Over all the screens and scrims the diagram of FUCHS *to* GOLD *to* GREENGLASS *to the* ROSENBERGS *spreads and duplicates itself like a cancer or octopus over the* ROSENBERG *memorabilia. In the darkness the juror selection drum begins to glow and spin.*

25

Act One

The CLERK *is spinning the juror drum. The audience is the jury. Dialogue is directed to them. On the screen is the legend:*
UNITED STATES DISTRICT COURT, SOUTHERN DISTRICT OF NEW YORK

The United States of America v. Julius Rosenberg and Ethel Rosenberg, et al. *Before Hon. Irving R. Kaufman, D.J., and a Jury, New York, March 6, 1951, 10:30 o'clock* A.M.

Slowly the American flag covers the area.

STAGE A

BAILIFF No talking, please, or reading or gum chewing. Please rise.

Hear Ye, Hear Ye: Facing the flag of our country, acknowledging the principles for which it stands, this honorable United States District Court is now in session. The Honorable Irving R. Kaufman, Judge presiding. All persons having business before this court, draw near and ye shall be heard. God bless this United States District Court. Be seated.

THE GOVERNMENT The District Attorney moves the case for trial and is ready to proceed.

THE DEFENSE The defendants are ready to proceed.

THE COURT To the gentlemen in the jury box and to the ladies and gentlemen in the courtroom, I shall attempt to speak loud enough so that all of you can hear my questions. Do any of you know or have any of you had dealings, directly or indirectly,

26

with Irving H. Saypol, the United States Attorney for the Southern District of New York?

THE GOVERNMENT   Shall I rise?

THE COURT   Mr. Roy M. Cohn, would you rise please? I take it by your silence none of you knows any of these gentlemen who have risen. Does any juror know or has he had any dealings, either directly or indirectly, with Mr. Emanuel Bloch?

THE DEFENSE (*rising.*)   Representing Julius and Ethel Rosenberg.

THE COURT   Do any of you have any scruples against being a juror in a capital case?

Prospective jurors speak from the audience.

PROSPECTIVE JUROR NUMBER ONE   Your Honor, I am prejudiced somewhat against capital punishment and I have so stated in the Supreme Court of New York.

THE COURT   Very well. We will excuse you. Have any of you or any members of your family been in the armed forces of the United States?

FIRST JUROR   Yes, I had four brothers in the Army.

SECOND JUROR   Well, I had three brothers in the last war.

THIRD JUROR   I served in the Navy during the First World War.

FOURTH JUROR   My brother was in the service in the last war.

FIFTH JUROR   My brother also served in the Navy in the last war.

SIXTH JUROR   Yes, the United States Navy in the First World War.

SEVENTH JUROR   I had two brothers in the last war.

EIGHTH JUROR   I had two brothers and three nephews in the past war.

The Jury (*on the screen.*)

No. 1: (Foreman) Vincent J. Lebonitte Residence: White Plains, New York. A manager for an R. H. Macy branch in that suburb.

No. 2: Richard Booth   A caterer for a tennis club in Forest Hills, Long Island, called the Seminole Club.

27

No. 3: Howard G. Becker   Residence: Mamaroneck, New York. An auditor for the Irving Trust Company for twenty-four years.

No. 4: James A. Gibbons   An accountant for the New York City Omnibus Company for twenty-eight years.

No. 5: Charles W. Christie   An auditor for the Tidewater Associated Oil Company, which had "contracts with the Government" to do war work.

No. 6: Harold H. Axley   A restaurant owner previously employed as a civilian expert in the finance department of the Army from 1942 to 1946.

No. 7: Emanuel Clarence Dean (Negro)   Eleven-year employee of the Consolidated Edison Company.

No. 8: Chauncey E. Miller   Residence: Scarsdale, New York. A secretary of the Board of Commissioners of Pilots, an agency of the State of New York, for twenty years. A member of the American Legion.

No. 9: Mrs. Lisette D. Dammas   Served on Bronx County Grand Jury in May, 1950. Son-in-law in National Guard.

No. 10: Charles J. Duda   Residence: Dobbs Ferry, New York. A bookkeeper for Davis and Lawrence Company.

No. 11: James Mitchell   An accountant with Harris, Kerr, Foster and Company. When previously employed by the U.S. Post Office, he was passed by "the Loyalty Probe."

No. 12: James F. Tessitore   Residence: Mount Vernon, New York. An estimator for the Alco Gravure Division of Publications Corporation. During World War II, "printed millions of topics for the Government."

Alternate No. 1: John F. Moore   Residence: Bronx, New York. A business representative for the Consolidated Edison Company.

Alternate No. 2: Emerson C. Nein   Residence: Bronx, New York. An officer and auditor for the Empire State Bank.

Alternate No. 3: Richard Lombardi   Residence: White Plains Road. A Government employee (Post Office).

Alternate No. 4: Mrs. Edna Allen   Residence: Bronx, New York.

Husband employed by Consolidated Edison Company. Son in Army's Chemical Corps.

THE COURT (*to the audience.*) Thank you. Now has any member of the jury ever been a member of, made contributions to or been associated in any way with any of the following organizations, which are contained on a list published by the Attorney General pursuant to a Presidential executive order? Mr. Schaefer, would you please read page 33?

THE CLERK (*this is live and in media. The action overlaps.*) Abraham Lincoln Brigade, Abraham Lincoln School, Chicago, Illinois, Action Committee to Free Spain Now, American League against War and Fascism, American Association for Reconstruction in Yugoslavia, Inc., American Committee for Protection of Foreign Born, American Committee for a Democratic Greece, American Council on Soviet Relations, American Croatian Congress, American Jewish Labor Council, American League for Peace and Democracy, American Peace Mobilization, American Polish Labor Council, American Russian Institute of San Francisco, American Slav Congress, American Student Union, American Youth Congress, American Youth for Democracy, Armenian Progressive League of America, Boston School for Marxist Studies, California Labor School, Inc., 216 Market Street, San Francisco, California, Central Council of American Women of Croatian Descent, also known as Central Council of American Croatian Women, National Council of Croatian Women, Citizens Committee of the Upper West Side, New York City, Citizens Protective League, Citizens Committee to Free Earl Browder, Citizens Committee for Harry Bridges, *Comité Coordinador por República Española*, Committee for a Democratic Far Eastern Policy, Commonwealth College, Mena, Arkansas, Civil Rights Congress, and its stage affiliates, Committee to Aid the Fighting South, Communist Party, U.S.A., Communist Political Association, Connecticut State Youth Conference, Congress of American

29

Women, Council on African Affairs, Council for Pan American Revolutionary Writers, Council for Pan American Democracy, Daily Worker Press Club, Dennis Defense Committee, Friends of the Soviet Union, George Washington Carver School, New York City, German-American Bund, Hollywood Writers Mobilization for Defense, Hungarian-American Council for Democracy, Independent Socialist League, International Labor Defense, International Workers Order and affiliated groups, Jefferson School of Social Science, New York City, Jewish Peoples Committee, Joint Anti-Fascist Refugee Committee, Ku Klux Klan, Labor Research Association, Inc., Labor Youth League, League of American Writers, Macedonian-American Peoples League, Michigan Civil Rights Federation, National Committee for the Defense of Political Prisoners, National Committee to Win the Peace, National Council of Americans of Croatian Descent, National Council of American Soviet Friendship, National Federation for Constitutional Liberties, National Negro Congress, Nature Friends of America, Since 1939, Negro Labor Victory Committee, New Committee for Publication, Ohio School of Social Sciences, Peoples Educational Association, Peoples Institute of Applied Religion, Peoples Radio Foundation, Inc., Philadelphia School of Social Science and Art, Photo League, New York City, Proletarian Party of America, Revolutionary Workers League, Samuel Adams School, Boston, Massachusetts, School of Jewish Studies, New York City, Seattle Labor School, Seattle, Washington, Serbian Vidovdan Council, Silvershirt Legion of America, Slovenian-American Committee for European Workers Relief, Socialist Youth League, Southern Negro Youth Congress, Tom Paine School of Westchester, New York, United Committee for Democratic Rights, United Committee for South Slavic Americans, United Harlem Tenants and Consumer Organization, United May Day Committee, United Negro and Allied Veterans of America, Veterans against Discrimination of Civil Rights Congress of New York, Veterans of the Abraham Lincoln Brigade, Walt Whitman's School of Social Science, Newark, New Jersey, Washington Book Shop Association, Washington Committee for Democratic Action, Wisconsin Conference on Social Legislation, Workers Alliance, Workers Party, including Socialist Youth League, Young Communist League, Institute of Pacific Relations, American-Russian Institute for Cultural Relations with the Soviet Union, Inc., National Emergency Conference for Democratic Rights, China Aid Council, International Juridical Association.

There is a pause; THE COURT *resumes.*

THE COURT Now, in the first place, in the matter of punishment, your function is merely to pass upon the evidence. You add a column of figures; that is what you do. When you are through adding a column of figures you have a result.

To put it another way, the minds of the jurors should be the same as a white sheet of paper with nothing on it, with respect to this case, and you should only take the testimony as it comes from the witnesses and from no other source.

The grand jury has returned the indictment that will be read to you ultimately. I want you to know at the outset that the indictment is not evidence of guilt and should be entirely disregarded by you as evidence.

The defendants are presumed to be innocent until it is established beyond a reasonable doubt that they have offended against the law, as charged in the indictment. The defendants stand before you as any individual.

Do you subscribe to the principle that everyone, regardless of race, color, creed or position in society, and regardless also of his political or religious beliefs, is entitled to a fair trial, according to our laws?

Pause.

Has any juror any prejudice, bias or sympathy, based solely upon a person's educational background or personal appearance?

31

Pause.

Does any juror have any prejudice against the atomic bomb or information relating thereto, or object to the method employed by the Government of handling information concerning the atom bomb?

Pause.

Does any juror oppose use of atomic weapons in time of war or oppose the Government's continued research and development of atomic weapons?

Pause.

The following persons will be called as witnesses for the Government in this case.

Mr. Schaefer, would you please read them?

THE CLERK Dr. J. Robert Oppenheimer, Dr. Harold C. Urey, Dr. George B. Kistiakowsky, Dr. Anoch Lewest, Harry Gold, John Lansdale, Jr., Elizabeth T. Bentley, General Leslie R. Groves, David Greenglass . . .

STAGE B
RECONSTRUCTION (*THE GOVERNMENT AND THE PRESS, 1951*)

All Reconstructions are titled on the screen throughout.

A hurrying and frenetic group.

REPORTER Mr. Saypol, will you ask the death penalty in this case?

REPORTER Mr. Saypol, will you have to reveal any top secret information?

THE GOVERNMENT The Government's case will be documented by unimpeachable witnesses and evidence.

REPORTER Can you tell us who some of the——

THE GOVERNMENT There is a list of one hundred and twenty witnesses, and that includes some of this nation's top scientists.

REPORTER Atomic——

THE GOVERNMENT Top atomic scientists.

REPORTER Will Harry Gold be your top witness, Mr. Saypol?

THE GOVERNMENT There will be many famous names from all over the country.

REPORTER What about the spy ring?

THE GOVERNMENT The Rosenberg Spy Ring has been smashed and there will be more arrests.

REPORTER There will be more arrests?

REPORTER Mr. Saypol, will it involve——

THE GOVERNMENT We have the masterminds of the ring and we will definitely go before the grand jury for more indictments as this roundup continues. Thank you, gentlemen.

STAGE A

THE CLERK Mrs. Ruth Greenglass, Ann H. Sidorovich, Rose Sobell, Louis Sobell, O. John Rogge, Louis Abel.

THE COURT Now, does any member of the jury know any of the persons whose names were called and who will be witnesses in this case? I gather by your silence that your answer is in the negative.

Pause.

Mr. Schaefer will now read to you the indictment in this case.

THE CLERK The grand jury charges:

1. On or about June 6, 1944, up to and including June 16, 1950, at the Southern District of New York, and elsewhere, Julius Rosenberg, Ethel Rosenberg, David Greenglass, the defendants herein, did, the United States of America then and there being at war, conspire, combine, confederate and agree with each other and with Harry Gold and Ruth Greenglass, named as co-conspirators but not as defendants, and with . . .

STAGE B

MAN IN THE STREET

The voice of the questioner, like that of the gods, is oracular and from the cosmos.

Do you prefer baseball or football?
ANSWER   Baseball.
ANSWER   Football.
ANSWER   Baseball.
ANSWER   Football.
ANSWER   Decline to state.

STAGE A

THE COURT   Now, we will hear the openings and then we will call your first witness. Will you keep your opening statements very brief? Proceed, Mr. Saypol.

THE GOVERNMENT   May it please your Honor, Mr. Foreman, ladies and gentlemen of the jury:

The facts, as they are developed before you here, will demonstrate that this case is one of unusual significance, of a conspiracy to commit espionage. It takes on added meaning where the defendants are charged with having participated in this conspiracy against our country at the most critical hours in our history, in time of war, around 1944.

The evidence will show that the loyalty and the allegiance of the Rosenbergs was not to our country, but to communism, communism in this country and communism throughout the world.

THE DEFENSE   If the Court pleases, I object to these remarks as irrelevant and I ask the Court to instruct the District Attorney to desist from making any remarks about communism, because communism is not on trial here. These defendants are charged with espionage.

THE GOVERNMENT   I object to this interruption.

THE DEFENSE   I beg your pardon, Mr. Saypol, but I am forced to do it.

THE COURT   Will somebody permit me to make a ruling here?

THE DEFENSE   That is correct, your Honor.

THE COURT   Mr. Saypol objects to your objection, and you answer his objection, and I can't make a ruling.

THE DEFENSE   I am making my objection.

THE COURT   The charge here is espionage. It is not that the defendants are members of the Communist Party or that they had any interest in communism. However, if the Government intends to establish that they did have an interest in communism, for the purpose of establishing a motive for what they were doing, I will, in due course, when that question arises, rule on that point.

THE GOVERNMENT   That is the purpose of my remarks.

THE DEFENSE   Defendants take exception to your Honor's statement.

THE COURT   Very well.

THE GOVERNMENT   (*to the jury.*)   I am sorry for the interruption.

THE COURT   Excuse me a moment, Mr. Saypol. I said that the charge was espionage; I want to correct that. The charge is conspiracy to commit espionage.

THE GOVERNMENT   Yes.

THE COURT   All right.

THE GOVERNMENT   I have said the evidence will show that the primary allegiance of these defendants was not to our country, but to communism, both national and international.

It will show that this love of communism and the Soviet Union soon led them into a Soviet espionage ring.

You will hear how Julius and Ethel Rosenberg reached into wartime projects and installations of the United States Government to obtain from people in the armed services and from people in positions of trust in our Government secret information, documents and material vital to the national defense of our country, so that they could hand this material directly to agents of the Soviet Union and speed it on its way to Russia. The most important scientific secrets ever known to mankind!

The evidence will reveal to you how the Rosenbergs persuaded David Greenglass, Mrs. Rosenberg's own brother, to play the

35

treacherous role of a modern Benedict Arnold, while wearing the uniform of the United States Army.

STAGE B

MAN IN THE STREET Do you approve of our involvement in the Korean War?

ANSWER Who are you?

ANSWER I think we're fighting for freedom in South Korea.

ANSWER We should win and get out.

ANSWER No comment.

ANSWER No comment.

STAGE A

THE COURT Mr. Saypol, you have passed your allotted time. Try to rush it along a little bit.

THE GOVERNMENT We will prove that the Rosenbergs stole, through David Greenglass, the one weapon *that might well hold the key to the survival of this nation, and means the peace of the world—the atomic bomb!*

There came a day, however, that a vigilant Federal Bureau of Investigation broke through the darkness of this insidious business and collected the evidence that would bring these culprits before the bar of justice, before an American jury like you. These defendants and their Soviet partners in crime had at their command various amounts of money, with which to finance the escape from American justice into safe havens behind the Iron Curtain of the members of this espionage ring. The evidence of the treasonable acts of these defendants you will find overwhelming.

The evidence will prove to you, not only beyond a reasonable doubt, but beyond any doubt, that these defendants have committed the most serious crime which can be committed against the people of this country.

This evidence will point to only one possible verdict on your part, that of guilty, as charged by the grand jury.

THE COURT Mr. Bloch.

THE DEFENSE If your Honor please, I move for a mistrial in this case upon the grounds that the opening statement of the learned United States Attorney was inflammatory in character and introduced an element which is not pertinent to the case or relevant to it, to wit, communism, and made other inflammatory and damaging statements which are not part and should not be part of an opening.

THE COURT Your motion is denied.

THE DEFENSE Exception.

THE COURT Mr. Bloch, proceed.

THE DEFENSE Ladies and gentlemen of the jury, I am going to be very, very brief.

THE COURT I can't hear you, Mr. Bloch.

THE DEFENSE What I would like to impress upon you now is to remember at all times the oath you took when you were sworn in as jurors. We ask you, we plead with you, don't be influenced by any bias or prejudice or hysteria.

This is a very grave crime that these defendants are charged with. Very grave. And this trial arises in a rather tense international atmosphere. And I think all of us delude ourselves that we believe that we are completely free from all those pressures and influences that every minute of the day are upon us.

May I repeat, and I hope you forgive me if I repeat, and I hope the Court will forgive me if I repeat at this time; all we ask of you is a fair shake in the American way. We ask you to keep your minds open. We ask you to judge these defendants, American citizens, as you would want to be judged yourself if you were sitting as a defendant.

Finally, I would like you, of course, to pay particular attention to the witnesses that appear here and judge the issues by what comes out of the witnesses' mouths. And in that connection pay very careful attention to the witness. Test yourself by the same standards which guide your conduct in your everyday affairs; is this the kind of person who is telling the truth? What motive has this person to say thus and so? And I want you to focus your attention particularly on these witnesses who we now hear will appear for the Government. One is David Greenglass, who is a defendant here and who has pleaded guilty. And I would like you to pay particular attention to the testimony of Harry Gold.

We come to you and say to you, don't be swayed by emotion. The defendants do not expect you to give a verdict on the basis of sympathy or passion or prejudice. We want you to use your mind and your reason. That is all we have a right to expect of you, but that much we have a right to expect, and we tell you that in our opinion by the time you have heard all of the evidence in this case, you will be convinced that these defendants, as they have contended at all times and as they now contend, are innocent of this crime, for which they are now being charged. So please keep your minds open.

STAGE B

MAN IN THE STREET   As a consumer, do you notice any decline in service?

ANSWER   Well, it's not so bad; I can't complain.

ANSWER   Could you repeat the question, please?

ANSWER   Not bad.

ANSWER   No.

ANSWER   I didn't get the question.

STAGE A

THE CLERK   Call David Greenglass to the stand.

He is sworn. All of the GREENGLASS *questioning is conducted for* THE GOVERNMENT *by* ROY COHN. *The volume and book numbers of the trial transcript from which testimony is quoted are flashed on the screen as each sequence begins. Here the citation is:* Volume I, Book II.

THE GOVERNMENT Mr. Greenglass, will you try to keep your voice up so the Court and jury can get the benefit of your testimony. Are you the David Greenglass who is named as a defendant in the indictment here on trial?

DAVID GREENGLASS I am.

THE GOVERNMENT That indictment charging conspiracy to commit espionage?

DAVID GREENGLASS Yes.

THE GOVERNMENT Have you entered a plea to that indictment?

DAVID GREENGLASS I have.

THE GOVERNMENT What is that plea?

DAVID GREENGLASS Guilty.

THE GOVERNMENT Now, prior to the time you were remanded to the custody of the United States Marshal, what was your home address?

DAVID GREENGLASS 265 Rivington Street.

THE GOVERNMENT Here in Manhattan?

DAVID GREENGLASS Yes.

THE GOVERNMENT How old are you?

DAVID GREENGLASS Twenty-nine.

THE GOVERNMENT When were you born?

DAVID GREENGLASS March 3, 1922.

THE GOVERNMENT Are your parents alive?

DAVID GREENGLASS My father is dead. My mother is alive.

THE GOVERNMENT Do you have any brothers and sisters?

DAVID GREENGLASS I have two brothers and one sister.

THE GOVERNMENT Your sister is the defendant Mrs. Ethel Greenglass Rosenberg, is that correct?

DAVID GREENGLASS That is true.

THE GOVERNMENT And another defendant, Julius Rosenberg, is your brother-in-law?

DAVID GREENGLASS That is true.

STAGE B

The screen: From the files of Emanuel Bloch, attorney for Julius Rosenberg.

FBI Do you know that your brother-in-law said you told him to supply information for Russia?

JULIUS ROSENBERG That couldn't be so; he'd have to be out of his mind to say things like that. Will you bring him here and let him tell me to my face?

FBI What if we bring him here, what will you do?

JULIUS ROSENBERG I'll call him a liar to his face. Look, gentlemen, at first you asked me to come down and give some information concerning my brother-in-law David Greenglass about some black market trouble he's supposed to be in. Now, you're trying to implicate me in something. I would-like to see a lawyer.

FBI How about a smoke? Just a few more questions; do you want some gum? Now, when did Greenglass come home on furlough from Los Alamos? You said "winter." Was that when you might have discussed this Russian espionage business?

JULIUS ROSENBERG No, you're trying to involve me and I want to get in touch with my lawyer.

FBI All right, a lawyer from Mr. Rabinowitz' office has been on the phone. Your wife must have called him.

JULIUS ROSENBERG Hello. Yes. I don't know.

To the FBI.

Am I under arrest?

An AGENT *replies* "no."

They say "no." Yes, I understand. Thanks. Good-bye.

To the FBI *as he leaves.*

Good-bye, gentlemen.

The AGENTS *look at each other as the lights fade.*

STAGE A

The screen: Volume I, Book II

40

THE GOVERNMENT   Is Mrs. Rosenberg older or younger than you are?

DAVID GREENGLASS   Older.

THE COURT   How much older is she?

DAVID GREENGLASS   Six years.

STAGE B
RECONSTRUCTION (ARREST, 1950)

ETHEL ROSENBERG *is walking out of the New York City Federal Court House. Two* AGENTS *appear.*

FIRST AGENT   Mrs. Rosenberg, you'll have to come with us—you're under arrest.

SECOND AGENT   Federal Bureau of Investigation, Special Agents.

ETHEL ROSENBERG   What? Do you have a warrant?

FIRST AGENT   We don't need one. Let's go upstairs.

ETHEL ROSENBERG   But I just left the grand jury up there. I was called to testify, that's all. My children are waiting for me. I have a three-year-old.

FIRST AGENT   Let's go.

ETHEL ROSENBERG   Why are you doing this—I came down here today of my own free will. My children are expecting me.

They walk into another area.

Listen, I have to phone my neighbor. She's watching the children for me.

FIRST AGENT   All right. Go ahead.

ETHEL ROSENBERG   Hello. Listen, don't show any alarm. Are the boys there? Listen, after I testified, as I'm walking out, two FBI agents meet me and they're holding me in the office here. Mr. Bloch's father is coming over, so maybe I'll know more later. I'll have him call you. Meanwhile, take the children over to my mother's. And listen, let me talk to Michael for a minute.

Pause.

Hello, Michael. Are you helping take care of Robbie? Listen, dear, Mommy has to stay downtown a while. What? Michael, do you remember what happened to Daddy? Well, dear——

She tries to block out the scream from the other end.

STAGE A

The screen: Volume I, Book II

THE GOVERNMENT Are you yourself married?

DAVID GREENGLASS I am.

THE GOVERNMENT Do you have any children?

DAVID GREENGLASS I have two. One is nine months old and one is four years old.

THE GOVERNMENT Where were you educated, Mr. Greenglass?

DAVID GREENGLASS I was educated in New York.

THE GOVERNMENT Would you tell us briefly the schools which you attended here in New York.

DAVID GREENGLASS I went to P.S. 4, P.S. 97, Haaren Aviation School, Brooklyn Polytechnic and Pratt Institute.

THE GOVERNMENT What field have you pursued since your graduation from public school?

DAVID GREENGLASS I am a machinist.

THE GOVERNMENT After you left school and prior to 1943, did you have any practical experience as a machinist?

DAVID GREENGLASS I did.

THE GOVERNMENT Here in New York?

DAVID GREENGLASS In New York.

THE GOVERNMENT Now, in 1943 did you enter the Army of the United States?

DAVID GREENGLASS I did.

THE COURT May I suggest, Mr. Cohn, that you stand back a little bit. It will help the witness to speak up.

THE GOVERNMENT All right. What rank did you hold?

DAVID GREENGLASS Private. Eventually I became a T/4 Sergeant.

THE GOVERNMENT Were you thereafter assigned to work as a machinist while in the Army?
DAVID GREENGLASS I was.
THE GOVERNMENT Where was that?
DAVID GREENGLASS Los Alamos, New Mexico.

STAGE B
RECONSTRUCTION (COURTSHIP, 1938)

Here begins the personal time chamber of ETHEL and JULIUS ROSENBERG. The slate is wiped clean and their story begins. Their lives, their family, children, friends; childhood and youth; schools and synagogues and all the banal imagery and music, politics of everyday life.

DAVID GREENGLASS Ethel, whatsisname is here.
ETHEL ROSENBERG Put on a shirt, please.
DAVID GREENGLASS Crissake!
JULIUS ROSENBERG (entering.) Hello, Dave. Hi.
ETHEL ROSENBERG Did you eat?
JULIUS ROSENBERG We'll have some chow mein afterward.
ETHEL ROSENBERG Good, I'll be ready in a minute.
JULIUS ROSENBERG Hot, huh? Why don't you take off your shirt, Dave?

Pause.

How'd the game come out?

DAVID shrugs.

So, what are you doing tonight?
DAVID GREENGLASS If I had any money I'd go to a show.
JULIUS ROSENBERG If I had any extra I'd sure give it to you, too.
DAVID GREENGLASS Yeah? How much you got?
JULIUS ROSENBERG Just enough for the dance and the——
DAVID GREENGLASS Chow mein. You see, you're all set. You should pay me some rent cause Ethel types all your college papers. Keeps me up all night. Fooling around.

43

JULIUS ROSENBERG You're right.

ETHEL *enters.*

ETHEL ROSENBERG Is Davey at it again?

DAVID *squeaks a love song.*

JULIUS ROSENBERG That's a pretty blouse. Listen, isn't there anything for him to take in a show?

ETHEL ROSENBERG Listen, Dave, I told you there's free folk-singing at the center.

He continues to make noises.

You act like a child. Now, stop it, David. You know why there's never any money around here, for you or anyone else.

DAVID GREENGLASS (*starts to sing "The International."*)

"Arise ye prisoners of starvation.
Arise ye wretched of the earth."

ETHEL'*s mother enters.*

TESSIE GREENGLASS Leave the child alone, Ettie. In this house forget all your books, please. Julius dear, you know what I mean?

STAGE A

The screen: Volume I, Book II.

THE GOVERNMENT While out at Los Alamos, did you come to learn the identity of any scientist working on atomic energy?

DAVID GREENGLASS I did get to know a number of scientists and some of world fame, for instance, Dr. Oppenheimer——

THE GOVERNMENT J. Robert Oppenheimer?

DAVID GREENGLASS That is right, and there was Niels Bohr, whom I first knew as Baker.

THE GOVERNMENT Did you know that Dr. Harold Urey was connected with the Manhattan Project?

44

DAVID GREENGLASS I did.

THE DEFENSE Your Honor, I will object to whether or not this witness knew some of the most renowned scientists unless it is related to the issues in this case.

THE GOVERNMENT I would be glad to state to your Honor that the name of each scientist will be directly related to the defendants in this case.

THE COURT Very well.

THE GOVERNMENT Now, did you ever have any discussion with your sister and Julius Rosenberg concerning the relative merits of our form of government and that of the Soviet Union?

THE DEFENSE Objected to as incompetent, irrelevant and immaterial, and upon the further ground that this will obviously lead to matters which may only tend to confuse the jury and inject inflammatory matter which will make it difficult or almost impossible for the jury to confine themselves to the real issue in the case.

THE COURT Objection overruled.

DAVID GREENGLASS Yes. They preferred socialism to capitalism.

THE COURT Which type of socialism?

DAVID GREENGLASS Russian socialism.

THE GOVERNMENT Mr. Greenglass, I think you told us your wife went out to Los Alamos to visit you in August of 1944. What did she say to you at that time?

DAVID GREENGLASS My wife said that while she was still in New York, Julius Rosenberg invited her to a wonderful dinner at their home at 10 Monroe Street. She came to dinner and later on there was a conversation between the three present, my wife, my sister and my brother-in-law. It went something like this: Ethel started the conversation by stating to Ruth that she must have noticed that she, Ethel, was no longer involved in Communist Party activities——

THE DEFENSE Now, if the Court please, this is just what I was afraid of, and I move to strike out any reference to Communist——

THE GOVERNMENT I object to it being struck out, your Honor,

45

on the ground that it is directly relevant to the charge in this indictment, which will emerge as this conversation unfolds.

THE COURT   I will overrule the objection.

THE DEFENSE   I respectfully except.

THE COURT   The mere fact that the word "communism" is mentioned does not taint all of the testimony and make it inadmissible if it is otherwise relevant.

THE DEFENSE   But apart from the lack of causal connection between Communist affiliations and sympathies . . .

THE COURT   Well, you have already stated your objection. You stated it yesterday, and you stated it, I believe, the day before, too.

THE DEFENSE   I think that is so, your Honor.

THE COURT   And I have your objection and I have made my ruling.

THE GOVERNMENT   Go ahead, Mr. Greenglass.

DAVID GREENGLASS   That they don't buy the *Daily Worker* anymore or attend meetings, club meetings. And the reason for this is that Julius has finally gotten to a point where he is doing what he wanted to do all along, which was that he was giving information to the Soviet Union. And Julius then went on to tell Ruth that I was working on the atomic bomb project at Los Alamos and that they would want me to give information to the Russians. My wife objected to this, but Ethel said . . .

STAGE B
RECONSTRUCTION (THE FAMILY, 1946)

JULIUS ROSENBERG   Ethel, your mother's here. Hello, Mom.

ETHEL   Hi, Momma, you're early.

TESSIE GREENGLASS   There's garbage in front of the building. It's filthy. (*Her speech is punctuated with Yiddish idioms.*)

JULIUS ROSENBERG   Is that so? It's usually very clean.

TESSIE GREENGLASS   I wouldn't know. Ethel, you look tired.

ETHEL ROSENBERG   Mother, will you have tea?

TESSIE GREENGLASS   I can't stay. I'm going to eat with David and

Ruthie. They insist. I just want to know before I give them the money: Julius, can my David make a living from this new shop? Are you looking after him?

JULIUS ROSENBERG   I hope so. The papers talk about things be ing——

TESSIE GREENGLASS   Don't talk to me about the papers. I'm asking about my David. Will you treat him like a real partner? He's never had a break, you know what I mean, Julius.

ETHEL ROSENBERG   Mother, sit down. I'll call the kids.

TESSIE GREENGLASS   I can't stay. So what do you think, Julius? Is there something in it for David? They want to have a family too, you know. Ruthie is a wonderful girl. They deserve the best. Julius, you know what I mean?

ETHEL ROSENBERG   Momma, we're all hopeful. The prospects look good if we can get enough capital. David will have to work hard and take the same chances as all the rest of us.

TESSIE GREENGLASS   Yeah. So what classes are you taking now?

JULIUS ROSENBERG   You should hear her play the guitar.

TESSIE GREENGLASS   The guitar? I never even had a class to learn to read. Never had a rest or vacation in forty years. You're telling me about work? And she was always singing somewhere in New Jersey.

ETHEL ROSENBERG   Give David and Ruth my love, Momma.

STAGE A

The screen: Volume I, Book II.

THE DEFENSE   May I ask your Honor to instruct the witness to raise his voice, please?

THE COURT   Yes, we had the same difficulty with the other witness.

THE DEFENSE   I think the acoustics in here are very bad. We had the same difficulty at the last trial.

THE GOVERNMENT   Did you have a furlough January 1, 1945?

DAVID GREENGLASS   I arrived home January 1, 1945.

THE GOVERNMENT After your arrival in New York did there come a time when you saw the defendant Julius Rosenberg?

DAVID GREENGLASS It was in the morning and he told me to write up this information at night, late at night, and he would be back the following morning to pick it up. And he told me to write it up, to write up anything that I knew about the atomic bomb.

THE GOVERNMENT Anything else?

DAVID GREENGLASS He gave me a description of the atom bomb.

THE GOVERNMENT Did you do any writing at that time?

DAVID GREENGLASS I wrote up the information he wanted that evening. It included sketches on the lens molds and how they were used in experiments.

THE GOVERNMENT Tell us exactly what you gave Rosenberg.

The stage is dark as the sketch goes on the screen. The dialogue continues in darkness.

DAVID GREENGLASS I gave him a sketch of the lens mold. I marked it A, B, C, and I defined what the markings meant.

THE DEFENSE Are you saying that Government's Exhibit 2 represented a true copy of the sketch that you turned over to Rosenberg?

DAVID GREENGLASS A refers to the curve of the lens; B is the frame; C shows approximately how wide it is.

THE GOVERNMENT Your Honor, may I pass it to the jury?

THE COURT Yes.

The sketch remains on the screen.

THE GOVERNMENT (*lights cross-fade.*) We have reached a good stopping place, your Honor. In that connection, bearing in mind how conscientious your Honor is with respect to maintaining a continuing calendar, Monday, March 19, my son gets married in the afternoon.

THE COURT Off the record.

Discussion off the record.

Well it sort of goes against the grain of my Scotch soul, but it looks like we have got to adjourn early today, so we will recess until Monday morning at ten thirty. I am going to ask you again, I am going to remind you again, not to discuss this case with anybody, not to permit anybody to discuss it with you. This case apparently will arouse a lot of interest in the newspapers. I know that you must, therefore, redouble your efforts not to read anything about it and not to watch anything on television that concerns itself with it, or listen to anything on the radio that concerns itself with it. So we will recess until ten thirty Monday morning. I want to compliment you on your record of promptness, and I hope that you keep it up, and I wish all of you a pleasant weekend.

STAGE B

MAN IN THE STREET What is your favorite TV show?
ANSWER I don't have one.
ANSWER "Milton Berle."
ANSWER "Berle."
ANSWER What's her name? "Lucy." No. "Howdy Doody."
ANSWER Are you kidding?

STAGE A

The screen: Volume I, Book III.

THE GOVERNMENT Now, Mr. Greenglass, I think you have already told us that this lens mold, along with other things constructed in your shop, were used in connection with experimentation on the atomic bomb; is that correct?
DAVID GREENGLASS They were.
THE GOVERNMENT By the way, did you have any conversation with Rosenberg concerning the writing on the descriptive material?
DAVID GREENGLASS I did. Julius came to the house and received this information, and my wife, in passing, remarked that the handwriting would be bad, and Julius said there was nothing

to worry about, as *Ethel* would type it up—retype the information.

THE GOVERNMENT Did you have any further conversation with Rosenberg on the occasion when you turned over this material?

DAVID GREENGLASS Not at—he asked me to come to dinner, my wife and myself, for an evening a few days later—I can't remember—a day or two later.

THE GOVERNMENT Now, I would like you to tell the Court and jury exactly what happened from the time you entered the apartment on that night until the time you left. By that I mean, tell us who was there, tell us what was said and by whom.

DAVID GREENGLASS When I got to the apartment with my wife, there was Julius and Ethel Rosenberg and a woman by the name of Ann Sidorovich.

THE DEFENSE What was that name?

DAVID GREENGLASS Ann Sidorovich.

THE GOVERNMENT Now, keep your voice up, Mr. Greenglass, and tell us exactly what happened on that evening, exactly what was said and by whom.

DAVID GREENGLASS Well, the early part of the evening we just sat around and spoke socially with Ann and the Rosenbergs, and then Ann Sidorovich left. It was at this point that Julius said that this is the woman who he thinks would come out to see us, who will come out to see us at Albuquerque, to receive information from myself.

THE GOVERNMENT What kind of information?

DAVID GREENGLASS On the atomic bomb. And she would probably be the one to come out to see us. We then ate supper and after supper there was more conversation, and during this conversation there was a tentative plan brought forth, to the effect that my wife would come out to Albuquerque to stay with me, and when this woman, Ann or somebody, would come out to see us, they would go to Denver, and in a motion picture theatre they would meet and exchange purses, my wife's purse having this information from Los Alamos, and of course, that is the way the information would be transmitted.

THE GOVERNMENT Now, was anything said about the reason for Ann Sidorovich being present at the Rosenbergs' home on that particular night when you were there?

DAVID GREENGLASS Yes, they wanted us to meet this Ann Sidorovich, so that we would know what she looked like; and that brought up a point, what if she does not come? So Julius said to my wife, "Well, I'll give you something so that you will be able to identify the person that does come."

THE GOVERNMENT In other words, if Ann Sidorovich would come, she knew what you looked like; you knew what she looked like; but if somebody else would come, this would be mutual identification; is that right?

THE DEFENSE Mr. Cohn, please don't repeat the answer.

THE GOVERNMENT If I do so, your Honor, it is for the purpose of clarity. Strange names are coming in. However, I won't do it.

THE DEFENSE You know why I don't want you to do it, because sometimes re-emphasis——

THE GOVERNMENT I will settle it by saying that I won't do it, your Honor. All right, go ahead.

DAVID GREENGLASS Well, Rosenberg and my wife and Ethel went into the kitchen and I was in the living room; and then a little while later, after they had been there about five minutes or so, they came out and my wife had in her hand a Jello box side.

THE DEFENSE Side?

THE GOVERNMENT Side.

THE DEFENSE S-i-d-e?

THE GOVERNMENT That's right. About what size Jello box, the small size?

DAVID GREENGLASS The kind you buy in your home.

THE GOVERNMENT Right.

DAVID GREENGLASS And it had been cut, and Julius had the other part to it, and when he came in with it, I said, "Oh, that is very clever," because I noticed how it fit, and he said, "The simplest things are the cleverest."

THE GOVERNMENT Now, let me see if I understand that. Your wife had one side; is that correct?

DAVID GREENGLASS That's right.

THE GOVERNMENT Who kept the other side?

DAVID GREENGLASS Julius had the other side.

THE GOVERNMENT Was there any conversation as to what would be done with these two sides?

DAVID GREENGLASS Well, my wife was to keep the side she had, and she was to use it for identification with the person who would come out to see us.

THE GOVERNMENT May this be marked for identification, please?

Marked Government's Exhibit 4 for identification.

Your Honor, at this point I would like—this will be quite important—to have the witness take this Jello box and cut the correct side into two parts, just as he remembers it was cut on that night, in January of 1945, and I would like to ask him to indicate to the Court and jury which side he kept and which side Rosenberg kept. May I do that?

THE COURT All right.

THE GOVERNMENT Will you take Government's Exhibit 4 for identification and this pair of scissors, and address yourself to the appropriate side and cut it into two pieces?

WITNESS *cuts exhibit.*

The side that was cut was one of the thin sides; is that correct?

DAVID GREENGLASS That's right; this is the side I had. (*Exhibiting.*)

THE GOVERNMENT That was the side you had?

DAVID GREENGLASS That's right.

THE GOVERNMENT May we have this marked for identification as Government's Exhibit 4-A?

Marked Government's Exhibit 4-A for identification.

Where did you last see this other side on that night?
DAVID GREENGLASS   In Julius' hand.
THE GOVERNMENT   May we have the other side marked as 4-B for identification, your Honor?

Marked Government's Exhibit 4-B for identification.

Now, Mr. Greenglass, did Ann Sidorovich ever come out to see you?
DAVID GREENGLASS   No, she did not.

STAGE B

ANN SIDOROVICH   My husband and I were at the grand jury and we gave them everything. Well, they had some sort of story all set up—it was the Greenglass story—and if my answers didn't go along with theirs, then I was lying. Well, they kept pounding on that meeting in January which I could not remember for the life of me. I'm just obstinate enough not to tell them that, unless I remember it myself. We were persecuted for several years by the FBI. We were under twenty-four-hour surveillance for over a year. We lost a great many friends. They would call my husband at work and get him out to the car and show him pictures and talk to him, I think simply to embarrass him. Now, I don't know if they honestly believed it. Maybe they did at first because it was so pat. It was a loose end and they would have felt better if I had confessed to it. Anyway, we were fortunate the people my husband worked with liked him or he would have been jobless for a long time. It was really a miracle his firm kept him on. That was really a miracle.

STAGE A

The screen: Volume I, Book III.

THE GOVERNMENT   Did somebody else come out to see you?
DAVID GREENGLASS   Yes.

THE GOVERNMENT Was it a man or woman?

DAVID GREENGLASS It was a man.

THE GOVERNMENT And when was this visit?

DAVID GREENGLASS First Sunday in June, 1945.

THE GOVERNMENT Did you at that time know the name of this man?

DAVID GREENGLASS I did not.

THE GOVERNMENT Do you now know his name?

DAVID GREENGLASS Yes, I do.

THE GOVERNMENT What is it?

DAVID GREENGLASS Harry Gold.

STAGE B

HARRY GOLD (*he speaks into a wire recorder.*) I had completely forgotten the David Greenglass incident. For the life of me I could not recall Greenglass' name, so here's what the FBI did: A list of twenty names was selected; first we eliminated the least likely ten; then we cut the list further; finally a group of the three most likely was chosen, and lo, Greenglass was at the top. For his wife's name we did likewise, and again, Ruth headed the list.

STAGE A

The screen: Volume I, Book III.

THE GOVERNMENT Will you tell us exactly what happened from the first minute you saw Gold?

The following is acted out on Stage B and echoes the testimony continuing on tape.

DAVID GREENGLASS There was a knock on the door and I opened it. We had just completed eating breakfast, and there was a man standing in the hallway who asked if I was Mr. Greenglass and I said "yes." He stepped through the door and he said "Julius sent me," and I said "oh," and walked to my wife's purse, took out the wallet and took out the matched piece of the Jello box.

Live testimony resumes on Stage A.

THE GOVERNMENT Mr. Greenglass, one thing I forgot to ask you about in connection with the meeting up at Rosenberg's apartment when you and your wife went there for dinner. After Ann Sidorovich had left the apartment, did you have a conversation with Mr. and Mrs. Rosenberg?

DAVID GREENGLASS Well, at this point Mr. and Mrs. Rosenberg told me they were very happy to have me come in with them on this espionage work and that now that I was in it there would be no worry about any money they gave to me; it was not a loan, it was money given to me because I was in this work—and that it was not a loan.

THE GOVERNMENT Did they say anything about the source of that money?

DAVID GREENGLASS They said it came from the Russians, who wanted me to have it.

THE GOVERNMENT Now, in September, 1945, after you returned to New York, did you see Julius Rosenberg?

DAVID GREENGLASS It was the morning after I came to New York.

THE GOVERNMENT Now, would you tell us what happened? Where did you see him?

DAVID GREENGLASS He came up to the apartment and he got me out of bed and we went into another room so my wife could dress.

THE GOVERNMENT What did he say to you?

DAVID GREENGLASS He said to me that he wanted to know what I had for him.

THE GOVERNMENT Did you tell him what you had for him?

DAVID GREENGLASS Yes. And I told him, "I think I have a pretty good—a pretty good description of the atom bomb."

THE GOVERNMENT The atom bomb itself?

DAVID GREENGLASS That's right.

The sketch, now marked Government's Exhibit 8, appears on screen while the testimony from a darkened Stage A continues.

THE GOVERNMENT I show you Government's Exhibit 8 for iden-

55

tification, Mr. Greenglass, and ask you to examine it and tell us whether or not that is a replica of the sketch, a cross-section of the atomic bomb.

DAVID GREENGLASS It is.

THE GOVERNMENT And how does that compare to the sketch you gave to Rosenberg in September, 1945?

DAVID GREENGLASS About the same thing. Maybe a little difference in size; that is all.

THE GOVERNMENT Except for the size?

DAVID GREENGLASS Yes.

THE GOVERNMENT It is the same?

DAVID GREENGLASS Yes.

THE GOVERNMENT We offer this in evidence, your Honor.

THE DEFENSE I object to it on the same ground I urged with respect to Government's Exhibit 2 and I now ask the Court to impound this exhibit so that it remains secret to the Court, the jury and counsel.

THE GOVERNMENT (SAYPOL) That is a rather strange request coming from the defendants.

THE DEFENSE Not a strange request coming from me at the present.

THE GOVERNMENT We have discussed that with the Court, as counsel knows, and I think nothing else need be said. If I had said it or my colleague, Mr. Cohn, had said it, there might have been some criticism.

THE COURT As a matter of fact, there might have been some question on appeal. I welcome the suggestion coming from the defense because it removes the question completely.

THE GOVERNMENT And I am happy to say that we join him.

THE GOVERNMENT (COHN) By the way, who was present when you handed the written material including this sketch over to Rosenberg?

DAVID GREENGLASS My wife, my sister, Julius and myself.

THE GOVERNMENT By your sister, you mean Mrs. Rosenberg?

DAVID GREENGLASS That is right.

THE GOVERNMENT Now during the three years from 1946 until

1949 did you see Rosenberg at business from time to time?

DAVID GREENGLASS Yes, every day almost.

THE GOVERNMENT Did you have any conversations with him relating to espionage activities?

DAVID GREENGLASS I did.

THE GOVERNMENT Would you tell us those conversations which you recall?

DAVID GREENGLASS Well, in '46 or '47 Julius Rosenberg made an offer to me to have the Russians pay for part of my schooling and the GI Bill of Rights to pay for the other part, and that I should go to college for the purpose of cultivating the friendships of people that I had known at Los Alamos and also to acquire new friendships with people who were in the field of research that are in those colleges, like physics and nuclear energy.

THE GOVERNMENT Did he mention any particular institutions which he desired to have you attend?

DAVID GREENGLASS Well, he would have wanted me to go to Chicago, University of Chicago, because there were people there that I had known at Los Alamos.

THE GOVERNMENT Did he mention any other institutions?

DAVID GREENGLASS M.I.T. and then later on N.Y.U.

THE GOVERNMENT Now, did you ever agree to go to any of these schools?

DAVID GREENGLASS I said I would try, but I never bothered.

STAGE B
RECONSTRUCTION (MOTHER, 1950)

TESSIE GREENGLASS Hello? Hello? Hello; is this Mr. Bloch? Who? Alexander Bloch? Is this Mr. Emanuel Bloch? You're his father? Listen, this is Ethel Rosenberg's mother. How should I be? I'm am old woman. I'm not a healthy woman and Ethel's children have been dumped on me. It costs money and I am not well. No, they've been here two days already. What? No, the little one grinds his teeth in his sleep. That's right. He won't move from the window, he's watching all day. And the

57

older one is a *vilde hya*, he's too wild. I just can't stand it.
What's that? No, listen, they have to use the toilet on the
landing and all the neighbors are complaining about the noise.
What? Yes, I know all about it. But what's she doing to
Davey? Will she save him? Why is she being so stupid? So
what would be so terrible if she backed up Davey's story? She
wouldn't be in this mess. What can you do? *Zionisten, So-
cialisten*. Yes, I know, I know. What? How can I take it easy?
I can't do nothing. I'm killed. Somebody should be taking care
of me. Well, I'm just warning you right now—if you don't
get those brats out of my house, I'm going to dump them at
the nearest police station.

STAGE B

*The screen: From the files of O. John Rogge, attorney for David
Greenglass.*

FBI Let's have this again. You say you met Harry Gold where?
Let's look at the picture again. You know he was arrested last
month and confessed? There's no need to protect him. He
came to see you in Albuquerque in 1945, didn't he?

DAVID GREENGLASS Albuquerque, New Mexico.

FBI Now, do you remember when?

Pause.

I said, do you remember when?

DAVID GREENGLASS Not too well.

FBI In June?

DAVID GREENGLASS O.K.

FBI Shall I put that in?

DAVID GREENGLASS Put it in.

FBI So he came to your place in Albuquerque in June of '45.
But then you told him to come back later. Because you weren't
ready yet, isn't that right?

DAVID GREENGLASS All right. Put that in. But, listen, my wife
wasn't in the room when this guy came to see me.

FBI What did Gold say about who sent him?

Pause.

"Julius sent me"—was it something like that?

Pause.

Shall I put that in?
DAVID GREENGLASS Put it in.
FBI Now back to the Jello box. Do you remember where Gold said he got his half of the Jello box or where you got yours?

Pause.

I said, do you remember this Jello box business now? Can you recall it? All right, let's go over it all again. You say you met Gold where?

STAGE B

HARRY GOLD (*He appears talking into his wire recorder.*) If an attorney is appointed for me I would like him to understand very clearly that I must continue to give information to the FBI freely, that he is to put no restrictions whatever on that . . . regardless whether he thinks it is damaging to me or not.

STAGE A

The screen: Volume I, Book III.

THE GOVERNMENT Now did Rosenberg ever say anything to you about any reward that he had received from the Russians?
DAVID GREENGLASS He stated that he had gotten a watch as a reward.
THE GOVERNMENT Did he show you that watch?
DAVID GREENGLASS He did.
THE GOVERNMENT Did he mention anything else that he or his wife received from the Russians as a reward?
DAVID GREENGLASS His wife received also a watch, a woman's watch, and I don't believe it was at the same time.

59

THE GOVERNMENT When were you told about a watch that Mrs. Rosenberg had received, do you remember that?

DAVID GREENGLASS I don't recall when that was but I do recall that my wife told me of it.

THE GOVERNMENT You got that information from your wife, is that right?

DAVID GREENGLASS That is right.

THE GOVERNMENT Now, was there anything else that they received which they told you about?

DAVID GREENGLASS I believe they told me they received a console table from the Russians.

THE GOVERNMENT A console table?

DAVID GREENGLASS That is right.

THE GOVERNMENT Did you ever see that table?

DAVID GREENGLASS I did.

THE GOVERNMENT At their home?

DAVID GREENGLASS I did.

THE GOVERNMENT Did you have a conversation with the Rosenbergs concerning that table?

DAVID GREENGLASS Yes, I did.

THE GOVERNMENT Now will you tell us what that conversation was in connection with this console table as best you can recall it?

DAVID GREENGLASS I admired the table and my wife asked Ethel when she bought a new piece of furniture; she said she had not bought it, she had gotten it as a gift and my wife said it was a very nice gift to get from a friend, and Julius said it was from his friend and it was a special kind of table, and he turned the table on its side to show why it was so special.

THE GOVERNMENT And what did he show you when he turned the table on its side?

DAVID GREENGLASS There was a portion of the table that was hollowed out for a lamp to fit underneath it so that the table could be used for photograph purposes, and he said when he used the table he darkened the room so that there would be no other light and he wouldn't be obvious to anyone looking in.

STAGE B
RECONSTRUCTION (LOVE, 1949)

JULIUS ROSENBERG That was great. Shall I call my mother to check on Michael and Robbie? No, it's too late. Listen, get the guitar. They raised a lot of money tonight, at least $2,500. Come on, E, play my favorite.

ETHEL ROSENBERG *(she tunes the guitar.)* Boy, is he a good guy. I could listen all night to him. Not too loud now, with your singing.

JULIUS ROSENBERG With just us I'm not embarrassed. O.K.?

JULIUS *and* ETHEL *sing two verses and the chorus of "Solidarity Forever," to the tune of the "Battle Hymn of the Republic."*

Great. Hey, you're as good as Leadbelly.

They dance.

In some ways, you're a lot better. You know what I mean?

ETHEL ROSENBERG It's like a holiday tonight, Mr. Rosenberg. It's been a long time, Julie.

JULIUS ROSENBERG I love you, honey.

ETHEL ROSENBERG I love you.

JULIUS *hums, off-key, as he starts to undress her and make love.*

Dear Julie, dear bunny.

STAGE A

The screen: Volume I, Book III.

THE GOVERNMENT Mr. Bloch may examine, your Honor.

THE DEFENSE Do you bear any affection for your brother Bernie?

DAVID GREENGLASS I do.

THE DEFENSE Do you bear any affection for your sister Ethel?

DAVID GREENGLASS I do.

THE DEFENSE You realize, do you not, that Ethel is being tried for conspiracy to commit espionage?

DAVID GREENGLASS I do.

THE DEFENSE And you realize the grave implications of that charge?

DAVID GREENGLASS I do.

THE DEFENSE And you realize the possible death penalty, in the event that Ethel is convicted by this jury, do you not?

DAVID GREENGLASS I do.

THE DEFENSE And you bear affection for her?

DAVID GREENGLASS I do.

THE DEFENSE This moment?

DAVID GREENGLASS At this moment——

THE DEFENSE And yesterday?

DAVID GREENGLASS And yesterday.

THE DEFENSE And the day before yesterday?

DAVID GREENGLASS And as far back as I ever met her and knew her.

STAGE B
RECONSTRUCTION (DREAMS, 1949)

ETHEL ROSENBERG . . . so in the dream, I'm all alone in the Hungarian bakery. That's it—I own the bakery or I have control over it. And that's it, I just walk around. Is this an eating dream? Oh, and my dress is too short, as if it had shrunk. But I don't mind. It's kind of . . . kind of sexy.

A long pause.

THE DOCTOR What about that?

ETHEL ROSENBERG This is not an eating dream. We haven't had sex in weeks. I was thinking the other day that if we could just get away. Maybe if I could get the kids into some free day camp in the country. You know what I mean?

Pause.

THE DOCTOR Do you want to go on?

62

ETHEL ROSENBERG It's like the dream. I'm alone in the bakery and I have control. If I didn't have the children I would have —what? Not control . . . no, if I weren't married, I wouldn't have any children and I'd have—what? What? Opportunities? Opportunities!

She groans.

You know, my problem is I don't know what my problem is.

THE DOCTOR What kind of "opportunities"?

ETHEL ROSENBERG I don't know. "Things." This is crazy; the kids are my whole life. Maybe that's my problem. My outside life used to be so full that I had to write out a schedule every week. I got up at six and practiced my music for an hour; went to work; at lunch hour I studied my scores; at night, lessons, rehearsal. I was really going to be something.

Pause.

I'm always saying I'm going to go back to singing or take up guitar, I don't know. I was supposed to be the big singer, an actress . . . everything.

Pause.

What does the bakery stand for?

THE DOCTOR Go on about the "opportunities," if you can.

ETHEL ROSENBERG The hour's up, isn't it? No, the Hungarian bakery has something to do with you. The dress, the whole thing. Remember, I made fun of your accent that time? That was a big day for me.

THE DOCTOR Ya, it's very painful for you to show anger.

ETHEL ROSENBERG It's time, no?

THE DOCTOR Ya, time. I think this dream has something to it. We see next time.

ETHEL ROSENBERG (*she opens her purse.*) Good-bye. Oh, by the way, I brought a sample of my poetry. Purely for analytic purposes, as they say. Well, good-bye. Listen, take care of your cold. I'll see you the same time on Tuesday? Right?

63

THE DOCTOR Right.

STAGE A

The screen: Volume I, Book III.

THE DEFENSE Mr. Greenglass, you were questioned many times without your lawyer, isn't that true?

DAVID GREENGLASS There were other times my lawyer was present. I don't remember whether it was the third time, fourth time or the fifteenth time.

THE DEFENSE Do you remember what you talked about to the FBI?

DAVID GREENGLASS When I came down to talk to the FBI I talked about a number of things; whatever their interrogation led to, it loosened the springs of my memory and I was able to remember things I had forgotten.

THE DEFENSE From the time you told your wife you were not interested in this work of espionage, until the next morning, did you consult with anybody?

DAVID GREENGLASS I consulted with memories and voices in my mind.

THE DEFENSE Are you aware that you are smiling?

DAVID GREENGLASS Not very.

THE DEFENSE Did you believe you were doing an honorable or a dishonorable thing?

DAVID GREENGLASS Well, I had a kind of hero-worship there and I did not want my hero to fail.

THE DEFENSE You say you had a hero-worship? Who was your hero?

DAVID GREENGLASS (*smiling.*) Julius Rosenberg.

STAGE B

HARRY GOLD I am absolutely fascinated by a man with ability and therefore I was fascinated by—or rather, attracted to— Klaus Fuchs. We were kindred souls, as good friends as it is possible for two men to be.

STAGE A

The screen: Volume I, Book III.

THE DEFENSE Now, were you given any reference books or textbooks, while you were in jail since your arrest, relating to any scientific matter?

DAVID GREENGLASS No, I didn't—nobody gave me any.

THE DEFENSE Did you read any scientific books while you have been in jail?

DAVID GREENGLASS Just science fiction.

THE DEFENSE That is, of course, not a basic theoretical journal, is it?

DAVID GREENGLASS No.

THE DEFENSE That is a popular kind of scientific periodical?

DAVID GREENGLASS That's right.

THE DEFENSE Now, Mr. Greenglass, I believe you testified that you graduated from high school here in New York City?

DAVID GREENGLASS Yes.

THE DEFENSE And I think you testified that you went to Brooklyn Polytech?

DAVID GREENGLASS Right.

THE DEFENSE How long did you go to Brooklyn Polytech?

DAVID GREENGLASS Six months.

THE DEFENSE And how many courses did you take during those six months?

DAVID GREENGLASS About eight different courses.

THE DEFENSE And did you fail——

THE GOVERNMENT I object to that, your Honor. What difference does it make?

THE DEFENSE I am coming to a new subject now, your Honor.

THE COURT I assume you are.

THE DEFENSE Yes, and I wish you will bear with me, because I am going to connect this up.

THE COURT All right.

THE GOVERNMENT Well, I will let Mr. Bloch finish his question.

65

That is as far as I will commit myself at the moment, your Honor.

THE COURT Right.

THE DEFENSE Did you fail in your subjects?

DAVID GREENGLASS I was young at the time, about eighteen, and I liked to play around more than I liked to go to school, so I cut classes almost the whole term. Simple.

THE DEFENSE How many of the eight courses that you took did you fail?

DAVID GREENGLASS I failed them all.

THE DEFENSE Did you ever get a degree in science?

DAVID GREENGLASS I did not get a degree.

THE DEFENSE Did you ever get a B.S.?

DAVID GREENGLASS I did not.

THE DEFENSE Did you ever get an engineering degree?

DAVID GREENGLASS I did not.

THE DEFENSE From any recognized institution?

DAVID GREENGLASS I did not.

THE DEFENSE Have you pursued any other organized and formal courses, held under the auspices of a recognized educational institution, apart from the Brooklyn Polytech and the Pratt Institute courses that you have mentioned you took?

DAVID GREENGLASS I did not.

THE DEFENSE Do you know anything about the basic theory of atomic energy?

DAVID GREENGLASS I know something about it, yes. I am no scientific—I am no scientific expert, but I know something about it.

THE DEFENSE Did you ever take courses in calculus?

DAVID GREENGLASS I did not.

THE DEFENSE Differential calculus?

DAVID GREENGLASS No.

THE DEFENSE Or thermodynamics?

DAVID GREENGLASS I did not.

THE DEFENSE Or nuclear physics?

DAVID GREENGLASS I did not.

THE DEFENSE   Or atomic physics?

DAVID GREENGLASS   I did not.

THE DEFENSE   Or quantum mechanics?

DAVID GREENGLASS   I did not.

THE DEFENSE   Or advanced calculus?

DAVID GREENGLASS   I did not.

THE COURT   What is this all about? I haven't heard anybody——

THE DEFENSE   Why, if the Court please——

THE COURT   I haven't heard anybody testify to your complete list.

THE DEFENSE   I wonder, if the Court please, if this might be a convenient place to stop?

THE COURT   Have you got much more to go, Mr. Bloch?

THE DEFENSE   I am afraid so.

THE COURT   Do you think perhaps if we give you a good substantial lunch period you might shorten it?

THE DEFENSE   I will try.

THE COURT   We will recess for an hour and a half for lunch, Mr. Bloch, and that should give you an opportunity to go over your notes and see whether you can shorten it in any respect. We will recess until two twenty-five.

STAGE B

MAN IN THE STREET   What is your opinion of the addition of the words "under God" to the Pledge of Allegiance?

ANSWER   No comment.

ANSWER   It's about time, you know what I mean?

ANSWER   Since when?

ANSWER   Leave me alone.

ANSWER   I say, God bless us.

STAGE A

The screen: Volume I, Book III.

THE DEFENSE   Now, while you were in business at 370 East Houston Street, did you have any quarrels with your brother-in-law Julius?

DAVID GREENGLASS   Only business quarrels. It didn't amount to anything.

THE DEFENSE   Now let us find out. Julius was the outside man, was he not?

DAVID GREENGLASS   That's right.

THE DEFENSE   He was the one who went out and tried to get orders, right?

DAVID GREENGLASS   That's correct.

THE DEFENSE   You were in the machine shop?

DAVID GREENGLASS   That's right.

THE DEFENSE   Working on the machines?

DAVID GREENGLASS   That's right.

THE DEFENSE   And you had a number of employees from time to time, did you not?

DAVID GREENGLASS   That's right.

THE DEFENSE   Now, weren't there repeated quarrels between you and Julius when Julius accused you of trying to be a boss and not working on machines?

DAVID GREENGLASS   There were quarrels of every type and every kind. I mean there was arguments over personality, there was arguments over money, there was arguments over the way the shop was run, there was arguments over the way the outside was run. It was quarrels, just business quarrels——

THE DEFENSE   Did you ever come to blows with Julius?

DAVID GREENGLASS   No, I didn't.

THE DEFENSE   Do you remember an incident when you were sitting in the corner candy store at Houston and Avenue D when your brother Bernie had to separate the both of you?

DAVID GREENGLASS   It slipped my mind.

THE DEFENSE   What slipped your mind?

DAVID GREENGLASS   I mean I didn't remember it.

THE DEFENSE   Do you remember it now?

DAVID GREENGLASS   I do.

THE DEFENSE   You don't?

DAVID GREENGLASS   I do.

THE DEFENSE   You do? Did you hit Julius?

DAVID GREENGLASS   I—I don't recall if I actually hit him.

THE DEFENSE   No more questions.

THE CLERK   Call Ruth Greenglass to the stand.

She is sworn.

The screen: Volume I, Book IV.

THE GOVERNMENT   Now, Mrs. Greenglass, will you keep your voice up so that all the members of the jury can hear you?

RUTH GREENGLASS   Yes.

THE GOVERNMENT   Where do you live, Mrs. Greenglass?

RUTH GREENGLASS   265 Rivington Street.

THE GOVERNMENT   And you are the wife of David Greenglass?

RUTH GREENGLASS   I am.

THE GOVERNMENT   Do you know that David Greenglass was named as a defendant in the indictment which is now on trial?

RUTH GREENGLASS   I do.

THE GOVERNMENT   And you know, do you not, that you are named as a co-conspirator but not as a defendant in that indictment?

RUTH GREENGLASS   Yes.

THE GOVERNMENT   Now, do you recall a time when your husband was inducted into the Army?

RUTH GREENGLASS   Yes.

THE GOVERNMENT   Now, I call your attention to the time in November, 1944. Were you at that time planning to go out and visit your husband in New Mexico?

RUTH GREENGLASS   Yes, I was.

THE GOVERNMENT   And prior to this time that you left New York did you have a conversation with the defendants Julius and Ethel Rosenberg?

RUTH GREENGLASS   Yes, I did.

THE GOVERNMENT   Now, will you state, as best you can recollect, the substance of that conversation?

RUTH GREENGLASS   Yes, Julius said that I might have noticed that for some time he and Ethel had not been actively pursuing any Communist Party activities, that they didn't buy the *Daily Worker* at the usual newsstand. . . .

69

STAGE B

MAN IN THE STREET   What do you think of the new "TV dinners"?

ANSWER   Stinks.

ANSWER   Well, they're fast.

ANSWER   What?

ANSWER   I like the chicken pie.

ANSWER   I like the beef.

STAGE A

The screen: Volume I, Book IV.

THE COURT   Madam, would you sit back?

RUTH GREENGLASS   Yes, I am sorry.

THE COURT   Just speak a little slower, please.

RUTH GREENGLASS   Yes.

THE DEFENSE   Now, Mrs. Greenglass, didn't something happen in 1949 that created hostility between you and the Rosenbergs?

RUTH GREENGLASS   No, there was no hostility.

THE DEFENSE   Did you ever visit the Pitt machine shop in 1949?

RUTH GREENGLASS   Yes. It was near my home. About five blocks. I used to go there with the carriage.

THE DEFENSE   Did you know that your husband and Mr. Rosenberg had had differences about the business that was being conducted there?

RUTH GREENGLASS   I heard that.

THE DEFENSE   Didn't your husband accuse Mr. Rosenberg of not treating him right?

RUTH GREENGLASS   My husband didn't accuse him of anything, Mr. Bloch.

THE DEFENSE   There were arguments, weren't there?

RUTH GREENGLASS   There weren't arguments. There were discussions.

THE DEFENSE   Didn't you complain to your mother-in-law and to other members of your family that your husband was being treated as a menial instead of one of the owners of the business?

70

RUTH GREENGLASS I said I didn't think my husband was being paid commensurate with the work done.

THE DEFENSE Was it on account of this friction that had occurred between your husband and Mr. Rosenberg that you stopped visiting them?

RUTH GREENGLASS No, Mr. Bloch, there was no friction involved. We had to have money for food and he had to go to work.

THE DEFENSE Are you hostile to either Mr. or Mrs. Rosenberg?

RUTH GREENGLASS No.

THE DEFENSE Are you friendly towards them?

RUTH GREENGLASS I have friendly feelings.

STAGE B

The screen: From the files of O. John Rogge, attorney for David Greenglass.

FBI Mrs. Greenglass, your husband seems to have his stories mixed up again.

RUTH GREENGLASS My husband lies when there's no reason for it. Sometimes he acts like a character in the movies. Last year he had—the doctor called it—a psychological heart attack. And once, he had a fever; he ran up and down the halls, in the nude, yelling "Lead pants, Elephant."

FBI (*very slowly.*) He says he wants to take back some of his confession . . . You know that'll mean going back out West to New Mexico on that uranium business . . . those stealing charges against him . . . and that's what we want to . . . avoid.

RUTH GREENGLASS You let me talk to him.

THE SCREEN

CONVICTED SPY, GOLD, IS STAR U.S. WITNESS

STAGE A

THE CLERK Call Harry Gold to the stand. Do you swear to tell the whole truth and nothing but the truth?

71

HARRY GOLD   I do.

SAYPOL conducts the GOLD questioning.

The screen: Volume I, Book IV.

THE GOVERNMENT   Now you are the Harry Gold, are you not, that is named as a co-conspirator in the indictment which is—in the indictment which includes the Rosenbergs?

HARRY GOLD   Yes, I am.

THE GOVERNMENT   Now do you stand convicted of any crime?

HARRY GOLD   Yes, I do.

THE GOVERNMENT   Of what crime?

HARRY GOLD   I stand convicted of espionage.

THE GOVERNMENT   What was the sentence that was imposed upon you?

HARRY GOLD   I was given a sentence of thirty years in the Federal Penitentiary.

THE GOVERNMENT   Now, did you meet Klaus Fuchs, Dr. Klaus Fuchs, some time in the middle of June, 1944?

HARRY GOLD   Yes, I did.

THE GOVERNMENT   Where did you meet Fuchs?

HARRY GOLD   I met Fuchs in Woodside, Queens.

THE GOVERNMENT   Did you have a conversation with Fuchs at this time? And what was the conversation?

HARRY GOLD   The conversation had to do with the fact that Fuchs had given me further information on the progress of the work going on in New York by a joint American and British project, which project was aimed at producing an atomic bomb.

THE SCREEN

This headline appears and remains until the end of the Act. The media are now beginning to throb with GOLD-*related thematic imagery. The comics and cartoons return.*

ATOM BOMB SHELTERS FOR CITY AT
COST OF $450,000,000 URGED

THE GOVERNMENT   Who was your Soviet superior at this time?

HARRY GOLD   Anatoli Yakovlev.

THE GOVERNMENT   Now, in May of 1945 did you have a meeting with Yakovlev?

HARRY GOLD   Yes, I did.

THE GOVERNMENT   Now, will you tell the jury what happened on this occasion?

HARRY GOLD   Yakovlev told me that he wanted me to go to Albuquerque, New Mexico. I protested. Yakovlev told me that I didn't understand that this was an extremely important business, that I just had to go to Albuquerque and he said, "That is an order," and that was all. I agreed to go. Yakovlev then gave me a sheet of paper; it was onionskin paper, and on it was typed the following: First the name "Greenglass," just "Greenglass." Then a number "High Street"; all that I can recall about the number is that the last figure—it was a low number and the last figure, the second figure was zero and the last figure was either five, seven, or nine; and then underneath that was "Albuquerque, New Mexico." The last thing that was on the paper was "Recognition signal. I come from Julius." In addition to this, Yakovlev gave me a piece of cardboard, which appeared to have been cut from a packaged food of some sort. It was cut in an odd shape and Yakovlev told me that the man, Greenglass, whom I would meet in Albuquerque would have the matching piece of cardboard.

THE GOVERNMENT   Now will you tell the jury about your last contact with Yakovlev?

HARRY GOLD   Yakovlev called me and said he would meet me at the Earl Theatre in the Bronx at eight o'clock that night. At exactly eight o'clock I was in the upstairs lounge of the Earl Theatre.

THE GOVERNMENT   What happened there?

HARRY GOLD   There I was accosted by a man. The man who met me was not Yakovlev. He was tall, about six feet two, had blond hair and a very determined feature. He walked with a catlike stride, almost on the balls of his feet.

73

GOLD *leaves the courtroom. He poses and whispers.*

I first got involved in spying through Tom Black of Jersey City. He was a fantastic man. He coiled a pet black snake around his neck and he had a trained crow that he used to pitch marbles to. I got involved in order to get Black off my neck about joining the Communist Party. I didn't want to. I didn't like them —they were a bunch of wacked-up bohemians. Then there was Steve Swartz. A virtual giant; long arms, big feet, big . . .

All the time axes, from political to personal, are building.

I recall him distinctly. He was at least six foot—possibly six foot one—and had an extremely savage face, tough-looking face, a plug-ugly.

STAGE B

The screen: From the files of John D. M. Hamilton, attorney for Harry Gold.

FBI Didn't you have some recognition sign as between the two of you? Some sign?

HARRY GOLD Yes, we did. I believe that it involved the name of a man and was something on the order of Bob sent me or Benny sent me or John sent me or something like that.

FBI Then in this case you would've had to say "Julius sent me," huh?

HARRY GOLD Who's Julius?

Now the action builds, cross-cuts from whispers to screams at the end.

THE CLERK Abraham Lincoln Brigade, Abraham Lincoln School, Chicago, Illinois; Action Committee for Free Spain Now, American League against War and Fascism, American Association for Reconstruction in Yugoslavia, Inc., American Committee for Protection of Foreign Born, American Committee for a Democratic Greece, American Council on Soviet Relations,

American Croatian Congress, American Jewish Labor Council, American League for Peace and Democracy, American Peace Mobilization, American Polish Labor Council, American Russian Institute of San Francisco . . .

HARRY GOLD First I created a wife I did not have. Then there had to be children to go along with the wife, and they had to grow old—it's a wonder steam didn't come out of my ears sometimes. When I went on a mission for the Russians, I immediately turned a switch in my mind; and when I was done, I turned the switch again and I was once again Harry Gold—just a chemist.

RUTH GREENGLASS David! David!

She is following a running, nude DAVID GREENGLASS.

DAVID GREENGLASS Lead pants! Lead pants! *Elephant!*

They disappear. JULIUS *and* ETHEL ROSENBERG *stand transfixed in the midst of the rising madness.*

THE VOICE OF J. EDGAR HOOVER (*over the action.*) The unknown man simply had to be found.

HARRY GOLD In late January or early February of 1944, I received my instructions. I was to walk on an East Side street; I was to carry an extra pair of gloves in my hand and a book with a green binding. I was supposed to meet a man who would carry a tennis ball in his left hand. This was on a deserted street, alongside an excavation, and I saw a slim, boyish-looking man, wearing horn-rimmed glasses, and that was Klaus Fuchs. We were as close as any two men could be.

KLAUS FUCHS There are also other crimes I have committed that are not crimes in the eyes of the law. I used my Marxian philosophy to conceal my thoughts in two separate compartments. Looking back at it now, the best way is to call it controlled schizophrenia.

HARRY GOLD When I was done I turned the switch again and I was once again Harry Gold—just a chemist.

TESSIE GREENGLASS (*this is simultaneous.*) Hello? Hello? Hello;

75

is this Mr. Bloch? Who? Alexander Bloch? Is this Mr. Emanuel Bloch? You're his father? Listen, this is Ethel Rosenberg's mother. How should I be? I'm an old woman. I'm not a healthy woman and Ethel's children have been dumped on me. . . .

THE GOVERNMENT (*we hear or see a reprise of part of the prosecution's opening charge and* THE COURT. *This is simultaneous action.*) The evidence will come from witnesses and you will see and hear that the witnesses are telling the truth as each link in this chain is forged and put into place, by testimony, by documentary evidence. Testimony and documentary evidence which will point conclusively to one thing and one thing alone—the guilt of the defendants.

ROY COHN *appears and the* MAN IN THE STREET; *they all begin a total recapitulation. All of* THE GOVERNMENT *evidence is repeated on the screen.* JULIUS *and* ETHEL ROSENBERG *stand motionless in the center.*

HARRY GOLD   While riding in a trolley car one day in Philadelphia I met and fell in love with a beautiful girl named Helen, who had one brown eye and one blue eye. I tried to court her but a wealthy rival named Frank, whose uncle manufactured peanut-chew candy, beat me out.

THE CLERK   Call Harry Gold to the stand. Do you swear to tell the whole truth and nothing but the truth?

HARRY GOLD   I at one time considered marrying and the girl in question told me at one time that she didn't think I was really in love with her. She felt that I was too cold. What she didn't know was that what made me cold all over and especially down here was the thought that if we were married and this thing came to light, what then? But I lost her anyway to someone called Nigger Nate. Later I lost my wife to an elderly, rich real estate broker. I actually had no wife and two twin children. I was a bachelor and had always been one. (*Screaming.*) It was my mother I lived with. My father's name was Sam and so was my Soviet spy master.

DAVID GREENGLASS   *Elephant!* Lead pants! *Elephant!*

The FBI *chases* DAVID GREENGLASS. *The* AGENT *shouts repeatedly,* "Shall I put that in?"

GOLD *and* FUCHS *talk at once.*

HARRY GOLD Bob sent me, or Benny sent me, or John sent me . . .

KLAUS FUCHS (*continues to repeat.*) There are also other crimes I have committed . . .

THE VOICE OF J. EDGAR HOOVER (*over the action.*) *The unknown man simply had to be found.* . . .

HARRY GOLD (*repeating simultaneously until the end of the Act.*) We were as close as any two men could be. Nigger Nate, Nigger Nate. We were as close as any two men . . .

On the screen the formula $E = MC^2$ *alternates with* GREENGLASS' *sketch (Exhibit 8) until the blackout.*

THE VOICE OF JOSEPH MCCARTHY.

This is heard punctuating the action until the blackout.

I have here in my hand a list of two hundred and five.
I have here in my hand a list of fifty-seven.
I have here in my hand a list of ten.
I have here in my hand a list of one hundred and sixteen.
I have here in my hand a list of one hundred and twenty-one.
I have here in my hand a list of one hundred and six.

THE VOICE OF J. EDGAR HOOVER (*over* GREENGLASS *and* GOLD, *the voice repeats until blackout.*) The unknown man simply had to be found. . . . The bomb has been stolen. Find the thieves, find the thieves, find the thieves. . . .

HARRY GOLD (*he kneels and weeps.*) I always lent other people money. Even when I didn't know them or even if I had to borrow to do it.

He screams.

I was known as Raymond and Martin and Dave from Pittsburgh!

THE VOICE OF JOSEPH MCCARTHY These young men, these fine
  young men . . .

This is repeated over and over as the entire vocal chorus rises to
the blackout. The lunatic chorus involves, by now, the whole cast.
The time capsule roars with imagery. At the apogee, the atom
bomb wipes out all sound and imagery. There is dead silence. On
the screen there is a close-up of HARRY GOLD.

THE VOICE OF HARRY GOLD Who's Julius?

The picture freezes in the silence.

THE SCREEN

The Government's Exhibit 8 covers the screen during the inter-
mission. Before the beginning of the second act we again see the
disclaimer:

EVERY WORD YOU WILL HEAR OR SEE ON THIS
STAGE IS A DOCUMENTED QUOTATION FROM
TRIAL TRANSCRIPTS AND ORIGINAL SOURCES
OR A RECONSTRUCTION FROM ACTUAL EVENTS.

Act Two

The dim siren. On the dark stage the CHORUS *intones and the gods slowly appear to speak and then disappear into darkness.*

STAGE B

MAN IN THE STREET (*in darkness.*)   Freud, have mercy on us.

FREUD   The state has forbidden to the individual the practice of wrongdoing because it desires to monopolize it itself. The warring state permits itself every misdeed, every act of violence. It practices deliberate lying and deception. The state exacts the utmost degree of obedience and sacrifice from its citizens, but at the same time treats them as children by maintaining an excess of secrecy, and a censorship of news. It leaves its citizens intellectually oppressed and defenseless against every unfavorable turn of events and every sinister rumor. The state makes unabashed confession of its lust for power, and the private individual is called upon to give his sanctions in the name of patriotism. Thus, all men suffer the feeling of blood-guilt.

MAN IN THE STREET (*in darkness.*)   Nietzsche, have mercy on us.

NIETZSCHE   Liberal institutions cease to be liberal as soon as they are attained: later on, there are no worse and no more thorough injurers of freedom than liberal institutions. . . . In the political realm hostility becomes spiritual. The new state needs enemies more than friends: in opposition alone does it feel itself necessary, only in opposition does it *become* necessary. And it is the same for the "internal enemy."

Thus all states are now ranged against each other: they presuppose their neighbors' bad faith and their own good faith. . . .

If the scientific *spirit* is lost, then all the fruits of science could not prevent a return to a state of superstition and witchcraft.

The whole problem of the Jews exists only in these same nation-states for here their energy and intelligence, their accumulated capital of spirit and will, gathered from generation to generation through a long schooling in suffering, has aroused mass envy and hatred. In all contemporary nations, therefore, the literary obscenity is spreading of leading the Jews to slaughter—as scapegoats of every conceivable public and internal misfortune.

Men are now called "free" so that they may be judged and punished—so that they may be made guilty.

Beware! Political superiority without any true human superiority is a calamity. It is time to make amends, to be ashamed of this false power!

MAN IN THE STREET (*in darkness.*) Marx, have mercy on us.
MARX The binding force of civilized society is the state. The state, that is, of the ruling class. A machine for keeping down the oppressed and exploited class. This state plays on the most sordid instincts and passions of mankind. Naked greed has been the moving spirit of the state from the first day of its existence to the present time.

In the highest form of the state, the democratic republic, wealth exercises its power indirectly, but all the more surely. Thus in the direct corruption of officials, America provides the classic example . . . now there is only one revolutionary emotion—shame.

Darkness.

MAN IN THE STREET Will an increase in the postal rate make any difference to you?
ANSWER No. . . .

ANSWER Certainly. . . .
ANSWER No. . . .
ANSWER No. . . .
ANSWER What?

STAGE A

THE CLERK Call Julius Rosenberg to the stand.

He is sworn. The screen: Volume II, Book I.

THE DEFENSE Now, Mr. Rosenberg, please keep your voice up. Don't make the same mistake some of the witnesses made and lower it as you go along. What is your full name?

JULIUS ROSENBERG Julius Rosenberg.

THE DEFENSE And how old are you?

JULIUS ROSENBERG Thirty-three.

THE DEFENSE Where were you born?

JULIUS ROSENBERG I was born in New York City.

THE DEFENSE Will you tell the Court and Jury the schools that you attended?

JULIUS ROSENBERG I attended Public School 88 on the Lower East Side in Manhattan, and then I attended Public School 96, a junior high school. At the same time I attended Hebrew School, the Downtown Talmud Torah. While I attended Seward Park High School, I attended Hebrew High School on East Broadway, New York. I entered the College of the City of New York in 1934.

THE DEFENSE Now, are you single or are you married?

JULIUS ROSENBERG I am married.

THE DEFENSE To whom are you married?

JULIUS ROSENBERG I am married to Ethel Rosenberg.

THE DEFENSE And as a result of that marriage did you have any children?

JULIUS ROSENBERG Yes.

THE DEFENSE What are the names of those children?

JULIUS ROSENBERG The oldest boy's name is Michael Allen Rosenberg.

81

THE DEFENSE   How old is he?

JULIUS ROSENBERG   He is eight years old. And the youngest, his name is Robert Harry Rosenberg.

THE DEFENSE   And how old is he?

JULIUS ROSENBERG   Four years old.

THE DEFENSE   Now, tell me, Mr. Rosenberg, you received an engineering degree, did you not?

JULIUS ROSENBERG   That is correct.

THE DEFENSE   Did you, in the course of your studies looking toward getting that degree, ever take courses in nuclear physics?

JULIUS ROSENBERG   I did not.

THE COURT   At any time prior to January, 1945, had anybody discussed with you, anybody at all, discussed with you the atom bomb?

JULIUS ROSENBERG   No, sir, they did not.

THE COURT   Did anybody discuss with you nuclear fission?

JULIUS ROSENBERG   No, sir.

THE COURT   Did anybody discuss with you any projects that had been going on in Germany?

JULIUS ROSENBERG   No, sir.

THE COURT   On the atom bomb?

JULIUS ROSENBERG   No, sir.

THE COURT   No?

JULIUS ROSENBERG   No, sir.

THE COURT   Did you ever discuss the respective preferences of economic systems between Russia and the United States?

JULIUS ROSENBERG   Well, your Honor, if you will let me answer that question in my own way, I want to explain that question.

THE COURT   Go ahead.

JULIUS ROSENBERG   First of all, I am not an expert on different economic systems, but in my normal social intercourse with my friends we discussed matters like that. And I believe there are merits in both systems, I mean from what I have been able to read and ascertain.

THE COURT   I am not talking about your belief today. I am talking about your belief at that time, in January, 1945.

JULIUS ROSENBERG Well, that is what I am talking about. At that time, what I believed at that time I still believe today. In the first place, I heartily approve our system of justice as performed in this country, Anglo-Saxon jurisprudence. I am in favor, heartily in favor, of our Constitution and Bill of Rights and I owe my allegiance to my country at all times.

THE DEFENSE Do you owe allegiance to any other country?

JULIUS ROSENBERG No, I do not.

THE DEFENSE Have you any divided allegiance?

JULIUS ROSENBERG I do not, and in discussing the merits of other forms of government, I discussed that with my friends on the basis of the performance of what they accomplished, and I felt that the Soviet government has improved the lot of the underdog there, has made a lot of progress in eliminating illiteracy, has done a lot of reconstruction work and built up a lot of resources, and at the same time I felt that they contributed a major share in destroying the Hitler beast who killed six million of my co-religionists, and I feel emotional about that thing.

THE DEFENSE Did you feel that way in 1945?

JULIUS ROSENBERG Yes, I felt that way in 1945.

THE DEFENSE Do you feel that way today?

JULIUS ROSENBERG I still feel that way.

THE COURT Did you approve the communistic system of Russia over the capitalistic system in this country?

JULIUS ROSENBERG I am not an expert on those things, your Honor, and I did not make any such direct statement.

THE COURT Did you ever make any comparisons, in the sense that the Court has asked you, about whether you preferred one system over another?

JULIUS ROSENBERG No, I did not. I would like to state that my personal opinions are that the people of every country should decide by themselves what kind of government they want. If the English want a king, it is their business. If the Russians want communism, it is their business. If the Americans want our form of government, it is our business. I feel that the majority of people should decide for themselves what kind of government they want.

STAGE B

MAN IN THE STREET   Do you vote for the man or the party?
ANSWER   The man.
ANSWER   The man.
ANSWER   The man.
ANSWER   Decline to state.

STAGE A

The screen: Volume II, Books I–II.

THE DEFENSE   Did you tell Ruth or Dave Greenglass that you were entertaining and spending $50 to $75 a night in connection with your espionage work?
JULIUS ROSENBERG   I didn't tell Dave or Ruth Greenglass or anybody that.
THE DEFENSE   Did you ever entertain anybody for any espionage work?
JULIUS ROSENBERG   I did not, sir.
THE DEFENSE   Tell me, how many suits have you bought for the last eleven years?
JULIUS ROSENBERG   About five suits.
THE DEFENSE   Did you come into court with a coat?
JULIUS ROSENBERG   Yes, sir.
THE DEFENSE   When did you buy that coat?
JULIUS ROSENBERG   I would say it was either 1941 or 1942.
THE DEFENSE   Did you ever buy a winter overcoat since then?
JULIUS ROSENBERG   No, sir. I did not.
THE DEFENSE   How much did you pay for that coat?
JULIUS ROSENBERG   Well, I estimate it was somewhere about $55.
THE DEFENSE   How much do you pay for your suits?
JULIUS ROSENBERG   About $26.
THE DEFENSE   Tell us what clothes you bought for your wife just roughly during this eleven-year period from 1940 to 1950.

JULIUS ROSENBERG When I got a per diem check once while working for the Government.

THE DEFENSE When was this?

JULIUS ROSENBERG I think it was about the same time I bought my coat, I bought her a fur coat.

THE DEFENSE How much did you pay for it?

JULIUS ROSENBERG Eighty dollars, and we remodeled it a couple of times and she still has it. Well, my wife bought her own clothes. I didn't buy her clothes for her.

THE DEFENSE Do you know about how much she spent on clothes for the last ten years?

JULIUS ROSENBERG Well, sir, I would estimate a maximum of about $300.

THE DEFENSE Mr. Rosenberg, you say you were aware of some trouble with stealing from the Army that David Greenglass may have been involved in when he was at Los Alamos in 1944?

JULIUS ROSENBERG That is correct.

THE DEFENSE When you heard he was being questioned by the FBI did you think it concerned this stealing?

JULIUS ROSENBERG I didn't know. It had been years before.

THE DEFENSE Will you describe what took place when David Greenglass approached you, in June of 1950, for help?

JULIUS ROSENBERG He asked me to meet him. He was very excited when——

STAGE B

DAVID GREENGLASS Julie, come on, where've you been? Come on, listen, will you?

JULIUS ROSENBERG Calm yourself, take it easy. What's troubling you?

DAVID GREENGLASS Julie, I'm in a terrible jam.

JULIUS ROSENBERG No—I realize you've been asking for money, you've been telling me to go to my doctor for a certificate, you've been talking about Mexico. What is the trouble, Dave?

DAVID GREENGLASS I can't tell you everything about it. All I

85

want you to do for me, Julie, is I gotta have a couple of thousand dollars in cash.

JULIUS ROSENBERG   David, I don't have that kind of money on me; I can't raise that kind of money.

DAVID GREENGLASS   Can you borrow it from your relatives?

JULIUS ROSENBERG   No, Dave, I can't do that.

DAVID GREENGLASS   Can you take it from the business for me?

JULIUS ROSENBERG   Dave, I cannot do that.

DAVID GREENGLASS   Well, Julie, I just got to have that money and if you don't get me that money you are going to be sorry.

JULIUS ROSENBERG   Look here, Dave, are you trying to threaten me or blackmail——

DAVID GREENGLASS   I'm warning you.

JULIUS ROSENBERG   Look, Dave, you go home and take a cold shower. You look like you're having an attack. I'm going to the shop.

GREENGLASS *leaves, mumbling to himself.*

STAGE A

The screen: Volume II, Book II.

JULIUS ROSENBERG   (*cross-fade.*)   Well, he was very excitable at this time, he was puffing and I saw a wild look in his eyes, and I realized it was time to cut this conversation short. I said, "Look, Dave, you go home, take a cold shower; I have some work to do. I am going to the shop; good-bye," and I left him at that time, and I made up my mind at that point that I wouldn't have anything to do with him, and I was very agitated.

THE DEFENSE   Did you give him any money?

JULIUS ROSENBERG   I did not give him any money.

THE DEFENSE   Did you give him any money at any time?

JULIUS ROSENBERG   No, I didn't.

THE DEFENSE   Mr. Rosenberg, to come back to the testimony that you spent $50 or $75 a night for entertainment: Have you ever been in a nightclub in your life?

JULIUS ROSENBERG   Once.

THE DEFENSE   What nightclub?

JULIUS ROSENBERG   Well, the Federation of Architects had a dinner party at Cafe Society.

THE DEFENSE   Was that the only nightclub you were ever at?

JULIUS ROSENBERG   That is the only nightclub I ever attended.

THE DEFENSE   Now, were you in the habit of going to high-class restaurants?

JULIUS ROSENBERG   I don't know what you mean by high class, Mr. Bloch.

THE DEFENSE   All right. Did you ever go to restaurants where the prices were expensive?

JULIUS ROSENBERG   Yes, I did.

THE DEFENSE   How many?

JULIUS ROSENBERG   Well, once when I was taking my wife out, to a place near Emerson Radio called Pappas, and on another occasion I have eaten at a place called Nicholaus on Second Avenue.

THE DEFENSE   Did you ever eat at Manny Wolf's?

JULIUS ROSENBERG   Yes. I remember eating there once.

THE DEFENSE   With whom?

JULIUS ROSENBERG   When I was working as an inspector at Jefferson Travers Radio they had a dinner party and they invited the inspectors down to Manny Wolf's for dinner and then for a show.

THE DEFENSE   Thank you. Your witness.

STAGE B

JULIUS ROSENBERG   ETHEL, I was terribly shocked to read that Willie McGee was executed. My heart is sad, my eyes are filled with tears. It seems to me that the federal courts have adopted the medieval practice of the Southern Bourbons, legal lynching of Negroes, and are now attempting, as in our case, to apply this to political prisoners. They must be answered with reason and fact.

I am positive growing numbers of people will come to understand our fight, and join with us to win so just a cause.

I miss you, Ethel, I love you. JULIE

STAGE A
IRVING SAYPOL *conducts all of* THE GOVERNMENT'S *questioning of the* ROSENBERGS.

The screen: Volume II, Book II.

THE GOVERNMENT Did you ever go out and collect any money for the Joint Anti-Fascist Refugee Committee?

JULIUS ROSENBERG I don't recall collecting any money, but I recall contributing money.

THE GOVERNMENT Do you remember at the time the agents arrested you? Did you ever see this before?

He flourishes a can and bangs it down on the jury rail.

May I read the label to the jury?

THE COURT Yes.

THE GOVERNMENT Will it be conceded that this is a can commonly used by solicitors for contributions?

THE DEFENSE I will so concede.

THE GOVERNMENT And the can reads on the label, "Save a Spanish Republican Child, *Volveremos*, We will return, Joint Anti-Fascist Refugee Committee, 192 Lexington Avenue, Suite 1501," and there is a notice on the back indicating that the City of New York permits these cans to be used for solicitation. So that perhaps you did a little more than just contribute?

THE DEFENSE Just a second, if your Honor please.

THE GOVERNMENT Is that so?

THE DEFENSE Wait a second: I object to the question. It presupposes a state of facts not proven. The can may have been found——

THE COURT Hold the question a moment. The witness wanted to say something.

JULIUS ROSENBERG That is not so, Mr. Saypol.

THE COURT What did you want to say?

JULIUS ROSENBERG The date on this can is May 20, 1949. I hold insurance in the International Workers Order, and they sent this can to me to solicit funds. I never solicited funds. I just made a contribution to them.

THE GOVERNMENT Do you know that the International Workers Order is now the subject of a lawsuit across the way in the Supreme Court?

THE DEFENSE I object to the question upon the ground it is incompetent, irrelevant and immaterial and not related to the issues in this case.

THE COURT What is the International Workers Order?

JULIUS ROSENBERG An insurance organization, your Honor.

THE COURT Is it a public insurance company?

JULIUS ROSENBERG Right, sir.

THE GOVERNMENT Is it not a fact that it is a Communist organization exclusively?

THE DEFENSE I object to the form of the question.

THE COURT The form is all right.

THE DEFENSE Do you want his opinion on it?

THE COURT Well, he certainly doesn't want mine.

THE DEFENSE He acknowledges that he belongs to it.

JULIUS ROSENBERG That is right, sir.

THE DEFENSE I think, if the Court please, we are really going off the issue.

THE COURT Oh, no!

STAGE B

MAN IN THE STREET What do you consider the greatest threat to our nation, today?

ANSWER Communism.

ANSWER Communism.

ANSWER Creeping socialism.

ANSWER Atheism.

ANSWER Decline to state.

Donald Freed • *Inquest*

STAGE A

The screen: Volume II, Book II.

THE GOVERNMENT Now you say you had another watch at some other time?

JULIUS ROSENBERG That is right, sir.

THE GOVERNMENT What kind of watch was that?

JULIUS ROSENBERG I remember the name——

THE GOVERNMENT Wasn't that name Omega, in a white metal case?

JULIUS ROSENBERG I believe that is the watch.

THE GOVERNMENT Is that the one you got from some Russian representative?

JULIUS ROSENBERG That is the one I got from my father.

STAGE B

JULIUS ROSENBERG MY DEAREST SWEETHEART, I've been reviewing past events of our lives. I remember when my father, a garment worker, was in a long strike against sweatshop conditions. Because he was a chairman and an active unionist, my father was blacklisted and had quite a pull to make ends meet. The constant battle against rats and vermin is still vivid in my . . .

STAGE A

THE COURT Do you believe in the overthrow of government by force and violence?

JULIUS ROSENBERG I do not.

THE COURT Do you believe—do you believe in anybody committing acts of espionage against his own country?

JULIUS ROSENBERG I do not believe that.

THE COURT Did you unhesitatingly express, in substance, the thoughts that you have just expressed about the Soviet government, the American government, to your friends and to your relatives?

90

THE GOVERNMENT Well, I submit, if your Honor please, just a moment ago in response to the Court's question the witness answered that he did not know enough about it and never talked to anybody about it.

THE COURT Well, do you presume to be an expert on government?

JULIUS ROSENBERG Well, I am not an expert but I talked about these matters.

THE COURT Have you read books?

JULIUS ROSENBERG Yes, some books I have read.

THE COURT Well, did you ever belong to any group that discussed the system of Russia?

JULIUS ROSENBERG Well, your Honor, if you are referring to political groups—is that what you are referring to?

THE COURT Any group.

JULIUS ROSENBERG Well, your Honor, I feel that at this time that I refuse to answer a question that might tend to incriminate me.

THE COURT Are you——

THE GOVERNMENT Just a moment. May I clarify that?

THE COURT It seems to me I have been hearing a lot about that.

JULIUS ROSENBERG Are you referring to membership in the Communist Party?

THE COURT Well, I am referring to membership in any political organization like the Communist Party.

THE DEFENSE And when you answered the Court's question did you have in mind the Communist Party?

JULIUS ROSENBERG Yes, I did.

THE COURT Well, now, I won't direct you at this point to answer; I will wait for the cross-examination.

STAGE B
RECONSTRUCTION (DECISION, 1951)

THE DEFENSE Let's take a minute, folks. I think they're going to push us on tomorrow afternoon.

JULIUS ROSENBERG Tomorrow?

91

THE DEFENSE It's a joke. They never intended to call Oppenheimer or Urey or— What's his name?

ETHEL ROSENBERG Who?

THE DEFENSE I'll think of it. Anyway we had to prepare anyway, just in case. Now, look, when we go on the stand; I spent the whole weekend debating what our approach should be. My father feels very strongly about it.

JULIUS ROSENBERG You mean about the Fifth Amendment?

THE DEFENSE That's it. Here's the point: this is a *political* trial——

JULIUS ROSENBERG I agree.

ETHEL ROSENBERG (*smiling.*) No.

THE DEFENSE Absolutely political, so we are going to have to take some chances. "Bring it out!" my father says. They have no evidence (let's keep our voices down), they haven't a thing so they're making communism the issue, right? So you deny Greenglass' lies and they come back—"Now, Mr. Rosenberg, did you ever belong to the Young Communist League a hundred years ago?"——

JULIUS ROSENBERG Or the Steinmetz Society at school.

ETHEL ROSENBERG This is ancient history.

JULIUS ROSENBERG Manny, you know—technically—they absolutely cannot prove any connection; we never actually——

THE DEFENSE Julie, that's not the point. They're going to try to hang us with the Fifth Amendment. I'm just telling you the advice I'm getting.

JULIUS ROSENBERG What?

THE DEFENSE That we should tell them what it was like to be poor in New York; a poor Jew, when you two were growing up. *There are no Jews on this jury!* In the meantime, there's three million Jews in this town, but we can't get a Jew on the jury.

ETHEL ROSENBERG And one woman. Saypol and Kaufman are——

THE DEFENSE Kaufman is murder. If I let myself go, I'll go to

jail for contempt, I'm telling you. He's ready to admonish me now. So, you go on the stand, we open up your whole lives. Why you believe in some kind of socialism, social justice, whatever. Then if they get cute and start red-baiting, we can call their bluff.

JULIUS ROSENBERG   When did you——

THE DEFENSE   I'm even seriously considering bringing your psychiatrist on, too. No?

ETHEL ROSENBERG   No. I'm sorry, that's out, Manny. But look, maybe Manny's right. With the Fifth Amendment we're damned if we do and we're damned if we don't.

JULIUS ROSENBERG   But we've got to stick to the evidence, phony as it is, don't you understand? If we answer just *one* question, then they can ask anything——

ETHEL ROSENBERG   But the jury might be more convinced if we——

JULIUS ROSENBERG   Honey, please, let's let Manny go over the——

ETHEL ROSENBERG   All right, I'm sorry.

JULIUS ROSENBERG   Please. We've got to destroy *their* own phony evidence. The jury——

THE DEFENSE   Let's look at it from their viewpoint. In a murder case, you know, the jurors might be guided by some damning physical evidence—a gun with fingerprints, clothing stained with the victim's blood. But what do they have here? Nothing. Just a story.

ETHEL ROSENBERG   I thought we were presumed to be innocent until——

JULIUS ROSENBERG   Very cute.

THE DEFENSE   All right. If I had anyone to help me, or any money for investigation or real research, we could go the other way. Maybe we could get Einstein on the stand, I don't know. But we're alone. The left—Ethel's family, for God's sake. We're alone and the country's hysterical. I just don't know which way to go. You wouldn't believe what's going on on

93

the outside. People who knew you—friends—take photographs from over the years and flush them down the toilet! No one wants to testify, people are getting passports.

JULIUS ROSENBERG But you always said, "We can't open the door." What's the use of a privilege if we don't use it?

Pause.

What time is it?

THE DEFENSE In other words, maybe I'm the wrong man for the case.

JULIUS ROSENBERG Manny, take it easy, Manny. Not so loud. They've got everybody fighting each other.

ETHEL ROSENBERG You know, this is all just like a dream to me. It's just rushing past. Rushing past and I don't understand anything. I just want to get it over with. Manny, tell me the truth about the children.

JULIUS ROSENBERG Lookit, we owe you our lives, but I'm afraid of it. If we don't take the Fifth Amendment, the FBI is going to testify that we were Communists. Who is the jury going to believe? Us or the FBI? But if we take the Fifth they can't pursue it. Can they? And the worst of all is if I don't take it, they're going to try to drag every name of everybody I ever knew or went to school with out of me. Not just names; *real people!* They'll make twenty spy rings before they're through. I'm afraid of it, Manny.

ETHEL ROSENBERG I don't understand a word; I think I'm losing my mind.

THE DEFENSE That's it. If you take it, then the jury says you're Reds anyway. If you deny membership, they could bring in some professional informer to say he saw you at some meeting and if the jury hears that, you'll be a liar in their eyes and you'll be fin——

Pause.

I'm so disgusted, I don't know. Maybe I'm kidding myself. All right, we'll see. Anyway, you and Ethel just be yourselves.

Don't worry about anything; I'm working on the situation with the children. *Oi*, Julie, Julie.

ETHEL ROSENBERG Listen, tell the children that we——

JULIUS ROSENBERG Listen, you take it easy, will you. You're driving yourself. You're only human, you know.

ETHEL ROSENBERG What if we——

GUARD Time.

STAGE A

The screen: Volume II, Book II.

THE GOVERNMENT Now, Mr. Bloch asked you the question and this was your answer: "Yes, I will, and in discussing the merits of other forms of government"—now this is you talking—"I discussed that with my friends on the basis of the performance of what they accomplished, and I felt that the Soviet government has improved the lot of the underdog there, has made a lot of progress in eliminating illiteracy, has done a lot of reconstruction work and built up a lot of resources, and at the same time I felt that they contributed a major share in destroying the Hitler beast." Then the Court asked this question——

THE DEFENSE Would you finish, please?

THE GOVERNMENT "The Hitler beast who killed six million of my co-religionists, and I feel emotional about that thing." Then later on the Court asked you this question: "Did you approve the communistic system of Russia over the capitalistic system in this country?" And you answered: "I'm not an expert on those things, your Honor, and I did not make any such direct statement." Do you remember having testified that way?

JULIUS ROSENBERG That's right.

THE GOVERNMENT Well now, you had said a little while before that you felt that "the Soviet government has improved the lot of the underdog there"; what did you mean by that?

JULIUS ROSENBERG What I read in newspapers.

THE GOVERNMENT And what did you read about the improve-

95

ment of the lot of the underdog in Soviet Russia, as you read it in the newspapers?

JULIUS ROSENBERG Well, that the worker there, as living standards were increased, his housing conditions were better than at times he lived under the Czar. That is what I mean by increasing the lot of the "underdog."

THE GOVERNMENT What newspapers did you read that in?

JULIUS ROSENBERG Various newspapers.

THE GOVERNMENT You mean the *Daily Worker*?

JULIUS ROSENBERG On occasion; *The New York Times*.

THE GOVERNMENT Any others?

JULIUS ROSENBERG Yes.

THE GOVERNMENT What others?

JULIUS ROSENBERG The *Herald Tribune*, the *World Telegram*.

THE GOVERNMENT The *Wall Street Journal*, perhaps?

JULIUS ROSENBERG No. I don't read the *Wall Street Journal*.

THE GOVERNMENT "Has made a lot of progress in eliminating illiteracy"; what did you know about that?

JULIUS ROSENBERG They built schools.

THE GOVERNMENT Where?

JULIUS ROSENBERG From what I read.

THE GOVERNMENT Where were the schools built?

JULIUS ROSENBERG In the Russian cities.

THE GOVERNMENT What cities?

JULIUS ROSENBERG I don't know, sir.

THE GOVERNMENT Where did you read that, same newspapers?

JULIUS ROSENBERG Newspapers.

THE GOVERNMENT "Has done a lot of reconstruction work"; what did you know about that?

JULIUS ROSENBERG Well, there are a lot of reporters that go to Russia and report how the cities have been rebuilt, that were destroyed by the Nazis.

THE GOVERNMENT What cities, for instance?

JULIUS ROSENBERG Stalingrad, Moscow.

THE GOVERNMENT What type of reconstruction had been done?

JULIUS ROSENBERG   I wouldn't know the details, sir. That is what I read the newspaper reports on.

THE GOVERNMENT   Has "built up a lot of resources"; tell me about the resources, won't you, please? What kind were they? Where were they? What they are? What were they intended for?

JULIUS ROSENBERG   I wouldn't know everything about it, but I knew they built some large dams. That is what I consider "resources."

THE GOVERNMENT   Dams you consider resources?

JULIUS ROSENBERG   That's right; hydroelectric stations. That is a dam.

THE GOVERNMENT   Did you read anything about the request of Russia for the atomic bomb? Would that be perhaps a resource that you had in mind?

JULIUS ROSENBERG   No, I was talking about a previous period.

THE GOVERNMENT   Did you tell the agents about your suspicions that David Greenglass had stolen uranium?

JULIUS ROSENBERG   Well, when a member of the family is in trouble, Mr. Saypol, you are not interested in sinking him.

THE COURT   Were you interested in protecting him at that time?

JULIUS ROSENBERG   Well, I felt that when a man is in trouble, the one thing his family should do is stick by the man, regardless of the trouble he is in.

THE COURT   Now, Mr. Rosenberg, why should David Greenglass come to you for help when you've testified that you had heated arguments over the business? Isn't it strange that he should come to you?

JULIUS ROSENBERG   I don't think so, your Honor, because in the first place his other brother was tied up with his wife dying in the hospital and——

THE GOVERNMENT   Did you tell us about that before?

JULIUS ROSENBERG   About what?

THE GOVERNMENT   About this wife who was dying and this brother who was out of the country and that is why you

97

thought you would go to him; that it was all right for him to call you to come to him.

JULIUS ROSENBERG I am only trying to understand why he came to me.

THE DEFENSE I object to the testimony. There is no testimony about a brother being out of the country.

THE GOVERNMENT Who was dying?

JULIUS ROSENBERG Bernie's wife.

THE COURT I think this subject matter, Mr. Saypol, is amply covered.

THE GOVERNMENT I never heard about this dying, whoever it was.

JULIUS ROSENBERG Well, Bernie's wife had Hodgkins' disease and was in and out of the hospital.

THE GOVERNMENT *Don't give us the gory details.*

Pause.

That is all—one question, if I may ask it?

THE COURT Pardon?

THE GOVERNMENT One question if I may ask it? Is or was your wife a member of the Communist Party?

JULIUS ROSENBERG I refuse to answer on the ground it might tend to incriminate me.

THE GOVERNMENT Very well, I don't intend to press it.

THE COURT Wait a minute. You are not going to press for an answer?

THE GOVERNMENT No, I don't think so.

THE COURT You may step down.

STAGE B

JULIUS ROSENBERG HELLO MY LOVE, You are so close at hand and yet your being in a different corridor separated by so much steel, locked away from my sight and beyond my hearing range the frustration is terrific. Tonight I was able to hear your voice when a few of the high notes of one of your arias was faintly audible . . . Physically I am fairly comfortable and already in the routine of things . . . I read about six newspapers a day, I play chess in a numbered board by remote control with another inmate and I am reading *The Old Country* by Sholom Aleichem. . . . Good night, my wife.

STAGE A

THE CLERK Call Ethel Rosenberg to the stand.

She is sworn. The screen: Volume II, Book II.

THE DEFENSE Are you married?

ETHEL ROSENBERG Yes.

THE DEFENSE To whom?

ETHEL ROSENBERG Julius Rosenberg.

THE DEFENSE The other defendant in this case?

ETHEL ROSENBERG That is right.

THE DEFENSE What was your maiden name?

ETHEL ROSENBERG Ethel Greenglass.

THE DEFENSE Will you kindly give the jury a brief sketch of your schooling and education?

ETHEL ROSENBERG Well, I attended Public School 22. And then I attended Public School 12. That was called junior high school. Then I attended Seward Park High School.

THE DEFENSE What, if any, other educational institutions did you attend?

ETHEL ROSENBERG I didn't go to any kind of institution but I had a private Hebrew tutor who came to the home. I also had a private piano teacher from whom I took lessons for about two years.

THE DEFENSE Did you also study voice?

ETHEL ROSENBERG Yes, I did.

THE DEFENSE With whom?

ETHEL ROSENBERG The Carnegie Hall Studios.

THE DEFENSE Anything else you studied?

ETHEL ROSENBERG Yes. When my child was about two and a half, I think, my older child, I took a course with the New School for Social Research in child psychology. I also took a

99

course in music for children at the Bank Street School in Greenwich Village, and then sometime in the spring of 1950 I took a course in guitar.

THE DEFENSE   Were these two courses, the one in child psychology and the other in music for children, taken in order to equip and condition you to raise your child?

ETHEL ROSENBERG   Yes, that really was the reason.

THE DEFENSE   How many children have you?

ETHEL ROSENBERG   I have two children.

THE DEFENSE   What are their ages?

ETHEL ROSENBERG   Well, Michael was eight March 10.

THE DEFENSE   He is the older of the two?

STAGE B
RECONSTRUCTION (CHILDREN, 1952)

On the dark stage we hear only THE VOICES OF THE CHILDREN.

THE VOICE OF MICHAEL   DEAR PRESIDENT EISENHOWER: My mommy and daddy are in prison in New York. My brother is six years old, his name is Robbie. Please let my mommy and daddy go and not let anything happen to them. If they come, Robbie and I will be very happy. We will thank you very much. Very truly yours, MICHAEL ROSENBERG

THE VOICE OF ROBBIE   I want to write one, too.

THE VOICE OF MICHAEL   No, I'm supposed to.

THE VOICE OF ROBBIE   I want to!

He starts a tantrum.

THE VOICE OF MICHAEL   Shut up! O.K. Tell me what you want to say and I'll write it down.

THE VOICE OF ROBBIE   O.K. You better.

Pause.

THE VOICE OF MICHAEL   Well, come on, Robbie.

THE VOICE OF ROBBIE   Shut up.

THE VOICE OF MICHAEL Then I'm——
THE VOICE OF ROBBIE DEAR MOMMY AND DADDY——
THE VOICE OF MICHAEL Robbie, you're supposed to write it to the President.

ROBBIE *begins to cry again.*

All right, go ahead then.
THE VOICE OF ROBBIE DEAR MOMMY AND DADDY . . .

There is a long pause.

STAGE A

The screen: Volume II, Book II.

THE DEFENSE Now, your brother Dave was the youngest in the family.
ETHEL ROSENBERG That's right.
THE DEFENSE What was your relationship?
ETHEL ROSENBERG Well, he was my baby brother.
THE DEFENSE Did you love him?
ETHEL ROSENBERG Yes, I loved him very much.
THE COURT Did he sort of look up to you?
ETHEL ROSENBERG Yes.
THE COURT And your husband? Before the arguments that were discussed here in court!
ETHEL ROSENBERG He liked us both. He liked my husband.
THE COURT Sort of hero-worship?
ETHEL ROSENBERG Oh, by no stretch of the imagination could you say that was hero-worship.
THE COURT You heard him so testify, did you not?
ETHEL ROSENBERG Yes, I did.
THE DEFENSE And it is not correct, is it, that there was any hero-worship there between Julius and your brother or your brother and Julius?
ETHEL ROSENBERG It certainly is not correct.
THE DEFENSE No. And when your brother went into the Army in 1943, you corresponded with him?

101

ETHEL ROSENBERG Yes.

THE DEFENSE And you also corresponded on behalf of your mother?

ETHEL ROSENBERG Yes, I did.

THE DEFENSE Your mother can't write English very well, can she?

ETHEL ROSENBERG No, she can just about sign her name.

THE DEFENSE So you were sort of a secretary on behalf of your mother?

ETHEL ROSENBERG Of both my mothers, yes.

THE DEFENSE And when your sister-in-law went to live with her husband, your brother, you continued writing to her?

ETHEL ROSENBERG Yes, I did.

THE DEFENSE Now, can you give us an idea of what you wrote about when you did write to your brother and to your sister-in-law?

ETHEL ROSENBERG Well, I wrote the usual "How are you? We are all right"; and "Take care of yourself"; and "This one had a baby," or "The other one got married," and things of that sort.

THE DEFENSE Did you ever, in any letter written to your brother or to your sister-in-law, refer to any matter pertaining to information concerning either the atomic bomb or any other instrument manufactured or used for national defense?

ETHEL ROSENBERG You mean, was there any such correspondence?

THE DEFENSE Did you ever write in any letter the substance of what I just now said?

ETHEL ROSENBERG Oh, no; no, I never did.

THE DEFENSE Tell me, did you ever know a man by the name of Yakovlev?

ETHEL ROSENBERG No, I never did.

THE DEFENSE Did you ever know a man by the name of Golos?

ETHEL ROSENBERG No, sir: I never did.

THE DEFENSE Did you ever know a woman named Bentley?

ETHEL ROSENBERG No, I never did.

THE DEFENSE Did you ever hear of those people at any time before this case broke?

ETHEL ROSENBERG I read about them in the newspapers.

THE DEFENSE Did you know a man by the name of Harry Gold?

ETHEL ROSENBERG No, I did not.

THE DEFENSE Did you know a man by the name of Fuchs, Dr. Fuchs?

ETHEL ROSENBERG Not until I saw his name in the newspaper.

THE DEFENSE And the same thing with Gold, you never knew of him until you read about it in the newspapers?

ETHEL ROSENBERG That is right.

THE DEFENSE Please describe the last time you saw your sister-in-law Ruth Greenglass.

ETHEL ROSENBERG After my brother was arrested, I waited for her one day at my mother's. She had the baby and we began to walk, she and I, with the carriage around the block.

STAGE B

The two women walk around the block as they talk.

RUTH GREENGLASS Let's not go far. Paper says rain.

ETHEL ROSENBERG Look, Ruth, I would like to know something: are you and Davey really mixed up in this horrible mess? You know how I have always felt toward Davey and how I have always felt toward you, although I must say you people haven't always reciprocated, especially in the last year. However, that is beside the point. I want you to know that even if you did do this, and Davey, my attitude toward you won't change. But I am his sister, and I have a right to know.

RUTH GREENGLASS What are you asking such silly questions for? He's not guilty and of course I'm not guilty and we've hired a lawyer and we're going to fight the case because we're not guilty. Did you think we were?

ETHEL ROSENBERG Look, I really don't know what to think any-more. There've been reports in the newspapers about confessions and much as I believed, always believed in Davey, I really began to wonder. I had to hear it from your own lips.

RUTH GREENGLASS Well, now you've heard it and it's the truth. Neither of us is guilty.

ETHEL *tries to embrace* RUTH.

ETHEL ROSENBERG I'll do whatever you say, Ruthie. Good-bye.

RUTH *rejects her.*

STAGE A

The screen: Volume II, Book II.

ETHEL ROSENBERG ". . . You can be sure I will do whatever I can," and with that we reached East Houston Street and I put my arms around her and kissed her. She remained rigid in my arms, didn't return the kiss, said, "Good-bye," coldly, turned on her heel and left.

THE DEFENSE That was the last talk you had with her?

ETHEL ROSENBERG That is right.

THE DEFENSE At the time of the arrest of your husband, where did you live?

ETHEL ROSENBERG Ten Monroe Street, Manhattan. In Knickerbocker Village.

THE DEFENSE Where are your children now?

ETHEL ROSENBERG (*beginning to break.*) They are at a temporary shelter in the Bronx.

THE DEFENSE Have you seen them since you were arrested?

ETHEL ROSENBERG No, I have not.

THE DEFENSE Your sister-in-law testified that she visited you at your home and that she admired a mahogany console table and she said "it was a very nice gift to get from a friend," and that "Julius said it was from his friend and it was a special kind of table" and thereupon your husband, Julius, "turned the table on its side to show us why it was so special"; did any such thing ever occur?

ETHEL ROSENBERG No, it did not.

THE DEFENSE Did your husband ever use any table, console table or any other table, for photograph purposes?

ETHEL ROSENBERG No, he did not.

THE DEFENSE Did your husband ever photograph on microfilm or any other substance anything pertaining to any information or secret concerning the national defense, or anything else at all?

ETHEL ROSENBERG No, he did not.

THE DEFENSE And did you, since the time you moved to the Monroe Street apartment until the time of your husband's arrest and your arrest, acquire any other tables?

ETHEL ROSENBERG Yes. We acquired a console table that my husband purchased at R. H. Macy. A very inexpensive table, with a back that you could . . . sometimes it would stand up, and other times if we wanted to use it for eating purposes, it folded down.

THE DEFENSE Did you ever hear Julius say to anyone that he got money from the Russians?

ETHEL ROSENBERG No, I never heard any such thing.

THE COURT Are you taking up every conversation that supposedly she had with Julius?

THE DEFENSE No, your Honor, I won't spend much more than a few minutes more to cover it.

THE COURT I don't want you to get the impression I am rushing you, but I don't want you to overtry a case, Mr. Bloch.

THE DEFENSE Did you ever hear from any source that Julius offered your brother and sister-in-law $75 or $100 a week to live on?

STAGE B
RECONSTRUCTION (MONEY, 1946)

JULIUS ROSENBERG (as ETHEL enters.) Hi, Dodgers won. Did you find anything in chairs, E? What's the matter now?

ETHEL ROSENBERG They're all way out of our price range.

JULIUS ROSENBERG Secondhand, too?

105

Pause.

What's the tragedy, Ethel?

ETHEL ROSENBERG Oh, what's the use? There's not any money for another baby and any new things for this house.

She looks in the mirror.

I can't stand this sweater! God's sake, I look twice my age!

JULIUS ROSENBERG Oh, come on, Ethel. Does everything have to be such a tragedy?

ETHEL ROSENBERG Stop saying that! Stop treating me like a case. I can't stand it. I don't have any clothes. I hate this place.

JULIUS ROSENBERG Well, what am I supposed to do about it?

ETHEL ROSENBERG Oh, shut up, will you?

JULIUS ROSENBERG Will you stop yelling, for God's sake, you'll wake the child.

ETHEL ROSENBERG You should never have married me. I'm sorry, Julius. I'm just so depressed over everything. You can't beat the system, that's all there is to it. I am never going to wear any of these sweaters again!

He goes to her.

Please, just leave me alone. It's not just furniture and clothes. There's just something wrong.

JULIUS ROSENBERG Listen, Ethel, money never meant that much to you. I mean, we're beyond that kind of thinking. You're just not getting enough from me. I mean that's it, isn't it?

Pause.

Will you please talk to me?

ETHEL ROSENBERG Oh, Julie, we have problems and I have problems. I have to solve my problems. Don't take it personally.

Pause.

I'm going to sleep with the child tonight in his room. I'm exhausted. Good night. I'm sorry.

STAGE A

The screen: Volume II, Book III.

THE GOVERNMENT Is it not a fact, Mrs. Greenglass, that before the grand jury——

ETHEL ROSENBERG Mrs. Rosenberg.

THE GOVERNMENT Excuse me, I'm sorry. You are the defendant here.

THE COURT Do you know, Mr. Saypol, if you could probably stand at the edge of the table there, we could all hear much better.

THE GOVERNMENT I am trying to save space and time.

THE COURT Go ahead.

THE GOVERNMENT Were you asked this question and did you give this answer before the grand jury?

"Did you invite your brother David and his wife to your home for dinner? I mean during the period while he was on furlough in January, 1945?"

"I decline to answer on the ground that this might incriminate me."

Do you remember giving that testimony?

ETHEL ROSENBERG Yes, I remember.

THE GOVERNMENT Was it true at the time you gave it? Yes or no.

ETHEL ROSENBERG It is not a question of it being true.

THE GOVERNMENT I would like to ask now that I have a categorical answer.

THE COURT Yes, will you answer that, please?

THE GOVERNMENT Yes or no.

ETHEL ROSENBERG What is the question?

THE COURT Was it true when you said that, that you refused to answer because it would incriminate you?

ETHEL ROSENBERG I said it might tend to incriminate me.

THE COURT Was that true?

THE DEFENSE I want to interpose an objection, your Honor.

107

THE COURT   Have you thought of another ground for an objection?

THE DEFENSE   I think, your Honor, that the method of trying to import an unlawful act to a person who has asserted the privilege against self-incrimination destroys the privilege and undermines and takes away the person's right under the Fifth Amendment, and I object to this entire line of inquiry because inferences may be drawn which are not warranted under the law or under the facts.

THE COURT   However, when a witness freely answers questions at a trial, the answers to the very same questions to which the witness had refused to answer previously upon a ground assigned by that witness, I ask you, is that not a question then for the jury to consider on the question of credibility? Nobody is seeking to destroy any privilege.

THE DEFENSE   May I just answer it in one sentence? I submit that I disagree with your Honor's conception of the law. What I meant was that the objective effect of it was to vitiate the rights.

THE COURT   But the witness herself has vitiated by giving answers to them at the trial, answers to these very questions.

THE DEFENSE   Well then, I submit, your Honor, that there is a failure to make, and I think I am putting my finger on the heart of this thing—there is a failure here to distinguish between the circumstances where a witness involuntarily appeared before a tribunal and is sworn to testify in response to a subpoena, as in the case here of a grand jury proceeding, and a case where the witness willingly takes——

THE COURT   Where is the witness willingly——

THE DEFENSE   Here. This witness has voluntarily taken the stand here. There was no obligation on her part to take the stand, your Honor.

THE COURT   Proceed.

ETHEL ROSENBERG   My brother had been arrested. My husband had been arrested.

THE GOVERNMENT   On August sixth?

ETHEL ROSENBERG My husband had been arrested and I had been subpoenaed to come before the grand jury. It was not for me to state what I thought or didn't think the Government might or might not have in the way of accusation against me.

THE GOVERNMENT What you are saying is that you were under no compulsion to confess your guilt in respect to this conspiracy?

ETHEL ROSENBERG I had no guilt——

THE DEFENSE Just a moment, please.

THE COURT She has answered.

ETHEL ROSENBERG *I had no guilt to confess!*

THE COURT But in your own interest I think you ought to think about it and give us some reason.

Pause.

STAGE B

MAN IN THE STREET What is your opinion on the so-called right of the Fifth Amendment?

ANSWER No comment.

ANSWER No comment, who the hell are you?

ANSWER They must have something to hide. Only the Commies want it.

ANSWER The what?

ANSWER No comment.

THE SCREEN

GRUNEWALD v. U.S., 77 S. CT. 963, OCTOBER 1956 TERM, p. 984 (OPINION OF JUSTICE BLACK CONCURRING WITH JUSTICES WARREN, DOUGLAS, AND BRENNAN):

"I CAN THINK OF NO SPECIAL CIRCUMSTANCES THAT WOULD JUSTIFY USE OF THE CONSTITUTIONAL PRIVILEGE TO DISCREDIT OR CONVICT A PERSON WHO ASSERTS IT. THE VALUE OF THE CONSTITUTIONAL PRIVILEGE IS LARGELY DE-

STROYED IF PERSONS CAN BE PENALIZED FOR
RELYING ON THEM.

"IT SEEMS PECULIARLY INCONGRUOUS AND IN-
DEFENSIBLE FOR COURTS WHICH EXIST AND
ACT UNDER THE CONSTITUTION TO DRAW IN-
FERENCE OF LACK OF HONESTY FROM THE
INVOCATION OF A PRIVILEGE DEEMED
WORTHY OF ENSHRINEMENT IN THE CONSTI-
TUTION."

STAGE A

The screen: Volume II, Book III.

THE GOVERNMENT Will you please tell me whether the answer,
when you gave it to the grand jury, as to whether or not you
had spoken to your brother David Greenglass to the effect that
the answer might tend to incriminate you, was true then or
false?

ETHEL ROSENBERG It was true, because my brother David was
under arrest.

THE GOVERNMENT How would that incriminate you, if you are
innocent?

THE DEFENSE Just a moment.

ETHEL ROSENBERG I didn't have——

THE DEFENSE Wait a second. I object to the form of the question.

THE COURT Let her give her own reasons to why she answered it
that way.

THE GOVERNMENT I am willing to have her explanation, if the
Court please.

THE COURT Yes.

ETHEL ROSENBERG It wouldn't necessarily incriminate me, but it
might——

THE GOVERNMENT You mean——

ETHEL ROSENBERG ——and as long as I had any idea that there

might be some chance for me to be incriminated I had the right to use that privilege.

THE COURT At any rate, you don't feel that way about that question today, do you? You have answered when you talked to your brother Dave right here in this courtroom, haven't you?

ETHEL ROSENBERG But I didn't talk to my brother David.

THE COURT What was the question there, Mr. Saypol? What was the question, please?

THE GOVERNMENT I am asking——

THE COURT No, no, the question you read before the grand jury; I want to know that question.

THE GOVERNMENT (reading.) "Q. Did you discuss this case with your brother David Greenglass? A. I refuse to answer on the ground that this might tend to incriminate me."

THE COURT You have no objection to answering that question here in the courtroom?

ETHEL ROSENBERG I have already answered that question, that I did not discuss it.

THE COURT And you don't feel that giving that answer will in any way incriminate you here today; is that right? That is why you have answered it?

ETHEL ROSENBERG That's right.

THE GOVERNMENT As a matter of fact, a truthful answer at that time would have been that you hadn't talked to him, would it not?

ETHEL Well, but self-incrimination——

THE DEFENSE Wait——

ETHEL (continuing.) Self-incrimination is not a truthful answer.

THE DEFENSE Wait. I just want to record my objection.

THE COURT I will sustain the objection to that particular question.

THE GOVERNMENT As a matter of fact, at the——

THE COURT Now, let me ask a question. If you had answered at that time that you had not spoken to David, for reasons best known to you, you felt that that would incriminate you?

ETHEL Well, if I used the privilege of self-incrimination at that

111

time, I must have felt that perhaps there might be something that might incriminate me in answering.

THE COURT   All right, proceed.

THE GOVERNMENT   As a matter of fact, at that time you didn't know how much the FBI knew about you and so you weren't taking any chances; isn't that it?

THE DEFENSE   I object to the form of the question.

ETHEL   I was using——

THE DEFENSE   Wait a second.

THE COURT   Overruled.

THE DEFENSE   I respectfully except.

THE GOVERNMENT   May that question be answered yes or no?

THE COURT   Yes, first answer it yes or no, then you can explain.

ETHEL   Will you please repeat the question?

THE GOVERNMENT   Mr. Reporter, will you please read the question?

Question read.

ETHEL   I didn't know what the FBI knew or didn't know.

THE GOVERNMENT   Of course you didn't, so you weren't taking any chance in implicating yourself or your husband.

THE DEFENSE   Now, if the Court please——

ETHEL   I was using my right——

THE DEFENSE   Wait a second. I object to this entire line of questions as incompetent, irrelevant and immaterial and I now move for a mistrial upon the ground that Mr. Saypol is persisting in asking questions, the import of which can only prejudice this defendant in the eyes of the jury, and it has no probative value whatsoever.

THE COURT   Mr. Bloch, you know the purpose of cross-examination, I take it?

THE DEFENSE   I do.

THE COURT   You know the way questions ordinarily are framed in cross-examination?

THE DEFENSE   I do, sir.

THE COURT   They don't expect a witness to volunteer and the cross-examiner has to phrase his questions in such a way as he thinks, with propriety, he can elicit the information which he thinks should be elicited. I think it is proper cross-examination. Your motion for a mistrial is denied. Your objection is overruled.

THE DEFENSE I respectfully except, your Honor.

THE GOVERNMENT Were you asked this question and did you give this answer:

"Do I understand you are going to decline to answer all questions that I ask you?"

"No, no I won't decline to answer all questions. It depends on the questions."

Did you say that?

ETHEL ROSENBERG Yes, I did.

THE GOVERNMENT When you said, "It depends on the questions," you meant it depends on whether or not the question and the answer that you gave would tend to incriminate you; is that right?

ETHEL ROSENBERG That is right.

THE GOVERNMENT You testified here today in response to questions from your counsel that the first time you saw Harry Gold was in this courtroom; is that so?

ETHEL ROSENBERG That is right.

THE GOVERNMENT Do you remember having been asked this question and giving this answer:

"Have you ever met Harry Gold?"

"I decline to answer on the ground that this might intimidate me, incriminate me, I mean."

Did you give that testimony at the time?

ETHEL ROSENBERG I gave that testimony.

THE GOVERNMENT Was that truthful?

ETHEL ROSENBERG When one uses the right of self-incrimination one does not mean that the answer is yes and one does not

113

mean that the answer is no. I simply refused to answer on the ground that the answer might incriminate me.

THE COURT   But you did answer it here in court, isn't that true?

ETHEL ROSENBERG   That is right.

THE COURT   And your answer here was that you never met him until he took the witness stand?

ETHEL ROSENBERG   That is correct.

THE GOVERNMENT   "Did you ever hear your husband, Julius, discuss with Ruth Greenglass the work her husband, David Greenglass, was doing at Los Alamos during the war?"

Answer: "I decline to answer on the ground that this might tend to incriminate me."

Was that testimony given by you?

ETHEL ROSENBERG   Yes.

THE GOVERNMENT   Was it truthful?

THE COURT   Same answer?

ETHEL ROSENBERG   Same answer.

THE GOVERNMENT   You profess a love for your brother, don't you?

ETHEL ROSENBERG   You mean I once had love for my brother?

THE GOVERNMENT   You mean that that has changed?

ETHEL ROSENBERG   It would be pretty unnatural if it hadn't changed.

THE GOVERNMENT   That will be all. The Government rests.

THE DEFENSE   The Defense rests.

May it please the Court, ladies and gentlemen of the jury. Two kinds of evidence came out of that witness box. One kind we lawyers call oral evidence. Then we have another kind that we call documentary evidence and those are what we call exhibits. Now what are the exhibits in this case? As we look through this entire pile of Government exhibits, we find nothing . . . but wait. We do have an exhibit, we have an exhibit here that ties Rosenberg up to the case. Here it is. It's a tin can. No question this came from Rosenberg's house. It says "Save A Spanish Republican Child" and it is issued pursuant to a license from the New York Welfare Department. I don't care whether you are in favor of Franco, and I don't care whether you are in favor of the Loyalists. But can you tell yourself in your conscience that there is anything in this can from which you can infer that Rosenberg was guilty of conspiracy to commit espionage? And finally, we have one last exhibit that connects the Rosenbergs in this case. It's a nominating petition signed by Ethel Rosenberg in 1941. As you can see, with many others she petitioned that Peter V. Cacchione could be nominated by the Communist Party so that he could run legally for office as a Councilman—to which office, incidentally, he was elected. Does signing that petition tie Ethel Rosenberg up with a conspiracy to commit espionage? Ask yourself that. The FBI stopped at nothing in their investigation to try to find some piece of evidence that you could feel, that you could see, that would tie the Rosenbergs up with this case. And yet this is the complete documentary evidence adduced by the Government. This case, therefore, against the Rosenbergs depends entirely upon oral testimony.

Now, here I want to say something to you. This case is packed with drama. Playwrights and movie script-writers could do a lot with a case like this. Now, who are the main actors here in this big drama? There is David Greenglass; there is Ruth Greenglass—that is one team, on this side; and in the other corner of the ring there is Julius Rosenberg and there is Ethel Rosenberg. You know, before I summed up, I went to a dictionary and I wanted to find a word that could describe a Dave Greenglass. I couldn't find it because I don't think that there is a word in the English vocabulary or in the dictionary of any civilization which can describe a character like Dave Greenglass. Now look at that terrible spy. (*He points to* ETHEL.) Look at that terrible spy and compare her to Ruthie Greenglass, who came here all dolled up, arrogant, smart, cute, eager-beaver, like a phonograph record. I say to you that this case started out to be a big, big case. It was going to last months, and it petered out in three weeks.

115

THE COURT   Your time is up, Mr. Bloch.

THE DEFENSE   I'm winding up now, your Honor. The fate of the defendants is in your hands. I have enough confidence in twelve American jurors to believe that they will bring in an honest verdict. That's all I ask you to do, to show to the world that in America a man can get a fair trial.

THE GOVERNMENT   May it please the Court, Mr. Foreman, ladies and gentlemen of the jury. This case is one of the most important that has ever been submitted to a jury in this country. I feel most inadequate to express to you in words the enormity of the thing. You have heard suggestions that the Federal Bureau of Investigation and my staff and I are silly dupes and we have been befogged, we have been fooled. If there had been any fooling, you will remember that one of the defendants made blanket negatives in denial as to whether she knew Harry Gold, as to whether she had ever talked to David Greenglass about his work at Los Alamos, as to whether she or her husband ever talked about atomic bombs, and yet I showed you that in the grand jury, on the advice of her counsel, she refused to answer those questions on the ground that to answer them would be self-incriminating.

In the grand jury: "Did you ever know Harry Gold?"

Answer: "I refuse to answer on the ground that it tends to incriminate me."

"Did you consult your counsel, Mr. Bloch, before you made that answer?"

Answer: "Yes."

I leave it to you as to who may have been fooled. The suggestion that the FBI has been duped? The FBI is never duped. The identity of some of the other traitors who sold their country down the river with Rosenberg remains undisclosed. We know that such people exist because of Rosenberg's boasting to Greenglass. We don't know all the details because the only

116

living people who can supply the details are the defendants. But there is one part of the scheme that we do know about. We know that these conspirators stole the most important scientific secrets ever known to mankind from this country and delivered them to the Soviet Union. The description of the atom bomb itself, destined for delivery to the Soviet Union, was typed up by the defendant Ethel Rosenberg. Just so had she on countless other occasions sat at that typewriter and struck the keys, blow by blow, against her own country in the interests of the Soviets. Ladies and gentlemen, every word that David and Ruth Greenglass spoke on this stand about that Jello box meeting was corroborated by Harry Gold. The history of this Jello box side, the greetings from Julius, and Greenglass' whereabouts in Albuquerque, New Mexico, come to us not only from Ruth and David, but from Harry Gold, a man concerning whom there cannot be even a suggestion of motive. He can gain nothing from testifying as he did in this courtroom except the moral satisfaction in his soul of having told the truth. Harry Gold, who furnished the absolute corroboration of the testimony of the Greenglasses, forged the necessary link in the chain that points indisputably to the guilt of the Rosenbergs.

THE SCREEN
CLIMAX OF TRIAL; JURY BEGINS TO DELIBERATE

STAGE B

JULIUS ROSENBERG Do you remember George Bernard Shaw's *Saint Joan*, Ethel? When John de Stogumber comes rushing in overcome with remorse for what he's done? "You don't know; you haven't seen; it is so easy to talk when you don't know. You madden yourself with words; you damn yourself because it feels grand to throw oil on the flaming hell of your own temper. But when it is brought home to you; when you see the thing you have done; when it's blinding your eyes, stifling your nostrils, tearing your heart, then—then, oh, God,

take away this sight from me! Oh, Christ, deliver me from this
fire that is consuming me—She cried to thee in the midst of it:
'Jesus! Jesus! Jesus!' She is in thy bosom, and I am in hell for
evermore."

STAGE A

THE COURT Bring the jury in.

THE CLERK How say you?

THE FOREMAN We the jury find Julius Rosenberg guilty as
charged. We the jury find Ethel Rosenberg guilty as charged.

THE COURT (*to the audience.*) Ladies and gentlemen of the
jury, I wish to tender you my deepest gratitude. I wish to con-
gratulate the Government for their fair presentation of this
case and again I say a great tribute is due to the FBI and Mr.
Hoover for the splendid job that they have done in this case.
Now I say to the jurors, I almost feel as if I will miss seeing
those faces here morning after morning, but I know it has been
a tremendous inconvenience to you; it has taken you away from
your business. God bless you all.

The ROSENBERGS *are brought before the bar for sentencing.*

The issue of punishment in this case is presented in a unique
framework of history. It is so difficult to make people realize
that this country is engaged in a life-and-death struggle with a
completely different system. This struggle is not only mani-
fested externally between these two forces but this case indi-
cates quite clearly that it also involves the employment by the
enemy of secret as well as overt outspoken forces among our
own people. All of our democratic institutions are, therefore,
directly involved in this great conflict. I believe that never at
any time in our history were we ever confronted to the same degree that we are today with such a challenge to our very existence. . . .

The punishment to be meted out in this case must therefore
serve the maximum interest for the preservation of our society
against these traitors in our midst. . . .

118

Certainly to a Russian national accused of a conspiracy to destroy Russia not one day would have been consumed in a trial. It is to America's credit that it took the pains and exerted the effort which it did in the trial of these defendants.

Julius and Ethel Rosenberg, I consider your crime worse than murder. Plain, deliberate, contemplated murder is dwarfed in magnitude by comparison with the crime you have committed.

The evidence indicated quite clearly that Julius Rosenberg was the prime mover in this conspiracy. However, let no mistake be made about the role which his wife, Ethel Rosenberg, played in this conspiracy. Instead of deterring him from pursuing his ignoble cause, she encouraged and assisted the cause. She was a mature woman—almost three years older than her husband and almost seven years older than her younger brother. She was a full-fledged partner in this crime.

Indeed the defendants Julius and Ethel Rosenberg placed their devotion to their causes above their own personal safety and were conscious that they were sacrificing their own children, should their misdeeds be detected—all of which did not deter them from pursuing their course. Love for their cause dominated their lives—it was even greater than their love for their children.

Your spying has already caused . . . the Communist aggression in Korea, with the resultant casualties exceeding fifty thousand and who knows but that millions more of innocent people must pay the price of your treason . . . by your betrayal you undoubtedly have altered the course of history to the disadvantage of our country . . . by immeasurably increasing the chances of atomic war, you may have condemned to death tens of millions of innocent people all over the world.

What I am about to say is not easy for me. I have deliberated for hours, days and nights. I have carefully weighed the evidence. Every nerve, every fiber of my body has been taxed. I am just as human as are the people who have given me the

119

power to impose sentence. I am convinced beyond any doubt of your guilt. I have searched my conscience—to find some reason for mercy—for it is only human to be merciful and it is natural to try to spare lives. I am convinced, however, that I would violate the solemn and sacred trust that the people of this land have placed in my hands were I to show leniency to the defendants Rosenberg.

It is not in my power, Julius and Ethel Rosenberg, to forgive you. Only the Lord can find mercy for what you have done. The sentence of the Court upon Julius and Ethel Rosenberg is, for the crime for which you have been convicted, you are hereby sentenced to the punishment of death, and it is ordered upon some day within the week beginning with Monday, May 21, you shall be executed according to law.

The screen: "The Pentagon Patriots."

THE CHORUS

"Now should this pair outwit the law
And wiggle from death's bloody maw;
An outraged nation with a yell
Shall drag them from the prison cell
        And hang them high
        Beyond life's hope,
        To swing and die
        And dangle from
        The Hangman's rope!
Then, while the buzzard's make a feast
On their Red flesh as on a beast;
Our natives shall rejoice and sing
And shout while these two traitors swing
And freedom's cry shall soar and swell
With songs that echo—'All is well!' "

STAGE B

The GUARDS *bring in the* ROSENBERGS *and lock them up. There are a half dozen* PRISONERS. *As* JULIUS ROSENBERG *passes one of the*

120

cells, he holds up two fingers and tries, unsuccessfully at first, to say, "Ethel, too." There is a long pause after the ROSENBERGS are put in cells at either end of the cell block.

PRISONER   Don't worry, Julie, you still got the appeal.

GUARD   Rosenberg, the Marshal's office upstairs says they're standing by for a message from Washington to take you up to Sing Sing tonight.

There is a long pause.

JULIUS ROSENBERG (calling.)   Ethel, don't be scared if some clown tells you we may be taken to the death house tonight! Everything will be all right; they can't do that.

There is another pause.

ETHEL ROSENBERG

Very simply and in true pitch she sings "Un bel dì vedremo," from Madama Butterfly, in Italian. The GUARDS and PRISONERS are still after she finishes.

GUARD (walks up to the cell of JULIUS ROSENBERG. They converse quietly.)   Rosenberg, I don't know about upstairs, but down here you're pretty damn lucky. Because of her.

JULIUS ROSENBERG   Thanks, but look at it this way. I just got the death sentence because I'm supposed to be the big shot in an espionage ring. I pass out $1,000 here, $1,500 there, toss $5,000 to my brother-in-law—but I never had the money to train that voice. I never had the money to do anything for her.

The PRISONERS call for encores.

ETHEL ROSENBERG (she begins to sing the "Battle-Hymn of the Republic." JULIUS joins her at the beginning of the next verse; at the same time their cells are clanged open and they are taken in opposite directions as the last phrase is heard and the lights fade.

121

> "O, be swift, my soul, to answer Him; be
> jubilant, my feet!
> Our God is marching on."

STAGE A

THE COURT   I want the motions very brief.

THE DEFENSE   Your Honor, tens upon tens of millions of people in this country, in Europe, in Asia, know about this case——

THE COURT   Yes, I want to say that I have been frankly hounded, pounded by vilification by pressurists. I think that it is not a mere accident that some people have been aroused in these countries. I think it has been by design. Yesterday, for instance, I received a barrage of telegrams.

THE DEFENSE   Your Honor, how is it that the Government, with thousands upon thousands of FBI agents, could not uncover one scrap of physical evidence so that you could be absolutely sure that these accusations are true?

THE COURT   Wasn't there some evidence about the table?

THE SCREEN

ARGUMENT BEFORE JUDGES SWAN, FRIENDLY, AND THURGOOD MARSHALL, DECEMBER 7, 1962, DOCKET NUMBER 27558

U.S. v. MORTON SOBELL, NUMBER 151, OCTOBER 1962

On the screen like lines of a play. The action is continuous:

JUSTICE MARSHALL   How would we rule today if the case being argued were that of Ethel Rosenberg instead of Morton Sobell?

UNITED STATES ATTORNEY   If Ethel Rosenberg were still alive— the bench would have to reverse her conviction.

STAGE A

THE DEFENSE   There is so much new evidence. We've found the console table if you would only look at it. Judge Kaufman, in your hands you have the fate of two human beings and you

122

must ask why in the shadow of death the Rosenbergs continue
to insist on their innocence. You know that they have read
the newspapers that we've all read. The newspapers that tell
them that if they would only talk, if they would only confess,
they would save themselves. What is it that stops them from
doing this?

THE COURT I have pondered that question. I have pondered it
over and over again, and the only solution I have to it is to
answer that it is the very same thing that drove them into it.

THE DEFENSE Your Honor, the reason they act this way is because
they are innocent. Believe me, they don't want to die; they are
in their middle thirties. They have been convicted on accomplice testimony that is highly suspicious to more and more
people. Surely there is at least some element of uncertainty,
your Honor. We can talk about the jury's verdict being proper;
this is not the quantum of proof that I am urging upon you
now. And I say, in all deference, that your Honor compounded
error when you made statements that I believe you probably
would not make today, namely, that it was the Rosenbergs who
caused the Korean War and the fifty thousand casualties.

THE COURT They were a contributing cause.

THE GOVERNMENT Your Honor, the Rosenberg Spy Ring, and
that alone, accounts for the stand which the Russians took in
Korea, which caused death and suffering to thousands of American boys, and I submit that these deaths and this suffering and
the rest of the state of the world must be attributed to the
tremendous contribution the Rosenbergs made. Now, if they
wanted to cooperate, they could give information that would
lead to the detection of any number of people. This is not the
time for a court to be soft with hard-boiled spies, when they
have showed no repentance and have stood steadfast in their
insistence on their innocence.

THE DEFENSE Your Honor, you must resist this war atmosphere.
I will get down on my knees here and now to beg you to spare
their lives, not just for their sake, but for their two little boys.

THE COURT I will reserve decision until later this week.

STAGE B

On the screen: *Lewisburg Penitentiary.*

HARRY GOLD   I am well. My weight is still at a normal 140 pounds and I don't ever intend to become sloppy fat again. Also a great source of satisfaction has been my work assignment here in medical research. A friend once said with much truth, just put Harry in a laboratory and he's happy. I've been reviewing my mathematics systematically and intensively—as I've intended for many years. I heard some of the World Series games over the radio here and we get football broadcasts over the weekend. Lately my "cup runneth over" since Penn beat Penn State.

STAGE B
RECONSTRUCTION (REUNION, 1951)

JULIUS and ETHEL ROSENBERG in prison, a screen between them.

ETHEL ROSENBERG   How did the kids seem to you, honey?

JULIUS ROSENBERG   When I came in the visiting room Michael was hiding under the table and the little one was asleep.

ETHEL ROSENBERG   Tell me.

JULIUS ROSENBERG   Robbie was asleep and Michael tackles my legs, you know. And then he started to open up a little.

ETHEL ROSENBERG   He did? Tell me.

JULIUS ROSENBERG   This'll kill you. He asked me if we had an *amicus curiae?* An *amicus curiae.* And then he says, did anyone besides Manny Bloch testify for you? That was it; then he closed right up.

ETHEL ROSENBERG   Well, that's something anyway. Sometimes I can hardly stand to even see them, and they know it. Do you think they understand, Julie?

JULIUS ROSENBERG   I hope so.

ETHEL ROSENBERG   Maybe to them I'm just another mother who runs away. You know for all they know all we have to do is say

what the Government wants and we could come home and all
be together again. They don't know from history and politics.
They're just lonesome. Oh, God——

JULIUS ROSENBERG You mean they don't know we're heroes? My
father the atom spy!

They both laugh.

Honey, honey, we've got to live up to the whole thing, a lot of
liberals are getting involved in the case, a lot of——

ETHEL ROSENBERG Do you know something, Julius? I can't even
worry about the liberals or anyone else. They'll do what they'll
do. I can't even think too much about the children (I know it
sounds terrible). But I am not a good German Jew and neither
are you, and I'm not going to be. That's what I'm holding on
to. I'm——

JULIUS ROSENBERG That's today. Last week it was "we're innocent and the people will save us." Wait a minute, let me talk,
I've got new reasons every day too: the kids, the Jews, world
peace, my hate for you know who, etc., etc. Sometimes I can't
even picture us ever going back to Knickerbocker Village, know
what I mean? Wait, let me finish, we've only got a minute. I
love you, that's the reason. I love you. Whoever invented celi-
bacy was insane. I'm making love to you, that's all my reasons.

*They talk at once and try again and again to kiss through the
screen.*

STAGE A

THE COURT I am again compelled to conclude that the defendants' guilt was established beyond doubt. Neither defendant
has seen fit to follow the course of Harry Gold and David
Greenglass. Their lips have remained sealed and they prefer the
glory which they believe will be theirs for their diabolical conspiracy. The defendants, still defiant, assert that they seek
justice, not mercy. What they seek they have attained. Application denied.

STAGE B

A VATICAN DIPLOMAT I am directed by the Holy See to inform the competent United States authorities that many new demands are being received at the Vatican urging the Holy Father to intervene for clemency in behalf of the Rosenbergs and that leftists' newspapers insist that his Holiness has done nothing. I will be most grateful if you will kindly notify this to the President. There is no doubt that when history returns to this episode, it will seal with a word of highest praise the magnanimous gesture of the Supreme Pontiff.

AN OLD WOMAN In the name of the family of Colonel Dreyfus, to whom world protest—including the people of America—and French justice assured vindication after a sentence obtained thanks to false testimony, forged documents and so-called confessions, we entreat you to prevent this irremediable act in order that the Rosenbergs be permitted the inevitable review of their trial.

VINCENZINA VANZETTI (*we see an old woman who speaks in Italian.*) Cosi spero fare onore e giustizia alla memoria di mio fratello Bartolomeo Vanzetti che, prima di morire, disse: "Io spero essere l'ultima vittima d'un ingiustizia tanto grande."

VINCENZINA VANZETTI (*simultaneous translation.*) I hope thus to honor and render justice to the memory of my brother, Bartolomeo Vanzetti, who, before dying, said: "I hope to be the last victim of such a great injustice."

THE SCREEN (simultaneous.)
U.S. v. GRUNEWALD, 233 F.2D 556. DECIDED APRIL 10, 1956 (FRANK DISSENT, WHICH THE SUPREME COURT UPHELD):

P. 576 "NO ONE WHO LEGITIMATELY EXERCISES THE CONSTITUTIONAL PRIVILEGE OUGHT TO BE SO PLACED THAT HE MUST SUBSEQUENTLY JUSTIFY IT TO A JURY."

P. 577 "AND AN UNFAVORABLE INFERENCE SHOULD NOT BE DRAWN FROM THE MERE FACT THAT THE FIFTH AMENDMENT PRIVILEGE HAS BEEN INVOKED."

PROFESSOR HAROLD C. UREY DEAR PRESIDENT EISENHOWER: Greenglass is supposed to have revealed to the Russians the secrets of the atomic bomb. A man of Greenglass' capacity is wholly incapable of transmitting the physics, chemistry and mathematics of the atomic bomb to anyone. New evidence makes even more plain what was plain enough before, that the prosecution's case has no logic in it, and that it depends upon the blowing up of patently perjured testimony.

Professor Albert Einstein joins me in begging you to spare the Rosenbergs. (Signed) Professor HAROLD C. UREY

DR. J. ROBERT OPPENHEIMER I was never requested to be a witness in the trial of Sobell or the Rosenbergs.

STAGE B
RECONSTRUCTION (DREAMS)

A wire screen separates them.

ETHEL ROSENBERG . . . but I'm not crying so much now. I still have that dream though.

Complete, hollow silence and the faint sound of birds.

THE DOCTOR Of the boy?
ETHEL ROSENBERG The scream on the phone when I told him. I'm dreaming about my mother lately, too.
THE DOCTOR What are your feelings?
ETHEL ROSENBERG None. That's the point. In one I'm just sitting watching her cook. She doesn't pay any attention to me and I have no feelings one way or another. But there's a lot of smoke, as if something were burning. What's wrong with me

127

that I still think of my mother and Davey as "family"? Why shouldn't I hate them?

THE DOCTOR   Why not?

ETHEL   Why shouldn't I hate them and love the people who've been more than a family to me? Wait a minute. I have a funny feeling right now. I feel anxiety.

THE DOCTOR   Go ahead.

ETHEL   I feel frightened, as if my mother could come right here into the prison and get me. Why can't I tell the truth about my feelings?

THE DOCTOR   Try.

ETHEL   What is there to be afraid of? It's the Government, not my mother, that's killing me. I love Manny Bloch as much as flesh and blood. I'm feeling very frightened now. I'm going to go on—I'm going on—the smoke in the kitchen! It's a smoke-screen. I feel love for you, too. Why not? You come all the way out here for nothing. You're kind, you never judge—

She is more and more emotional.

—in the kitchen, she'll take the knife and kill me! Doctor——

THE DOCTOR   (*he tries to touch her hand.*)   Ethel, can't you let them go?

ETHEL ROSENBERG   (*she struggles thought by thought.*)   I've got to. Who am I to judge anyone? I could save my children if I did what my mother says, "So what would be so bad, what would be so bad?" And Ruthie? So now she's just like my mother. That's what terrifies me—that I'm just like her too. There's only two choices when the Government picks your family out. Maybe if they'd come to us first I'd be Ruth Greenglass and Ruthie would have been Ethel Rosenberg. Listen, I know, I know.

THE DOCTOR   So, can you let them go?

ETHEL ROSENBERG   I'm letting the children go, God help me. There's been enough judging; I'm sick with it. Enough.

THE DOCTOR   Ya, ya.

ETHEL ROSENBERG   Well, what difference does it make now? Who

I hate, who I love? But I know that I would have made it. That's true, isn't it?

THE DOCTOR Before you were——

ETHEL ROSENBERG Before I was arrested, that summer, there was a real difference. I would have graduated, wouldn't I?

He laughs. They both laugh. Pause.

Did you know that I'm the only person in this whole building now?

THE DOCTOR Is that so?

Pause.

ETHEL ROSENBERG Listen to the birds.

Pause.

Yes, except for the matron. She's really a fine person. I like her very much. Very different backgrounds. In the old life we would never have met. You know New York is really a private little world, isn't it? I think we all miss a lot in life. Even though we think we're free. Was I really free then? I haven't mentioned Julius. I remember him as he looked when he was in college. And I love him truly. But the past is really gone, isn't it? Why should I hate anyone?

THE DOCTOR The past is still in your dreams.

ETHEL ROSENBERG But that's because it's gone. I know it's gone; otherwise I wouldn't feel so lonesome.

Screaming headlines, building toward the execution, begin. And the scenes of world protest. Now, through the theatre we hear the voices of JULIUS *and* ETHEL ROSENBERG. *As they make their appeal, the slow Ritual of Death begins. Their heads are shorn; their clothes rent. People enter and exit. There are secular and religious figures bending over them.* THE GOVERNMENT AGENT *creeps forward with the open-confession telephone to Washington. They are offered their last food and drink. Absolute silence except for the disembodied voices. Other* PRISONERS *stand frozen*

129

and listening. There are whispers everywhere: "Talk," "Tell us the names." The transaction becomes ambiguous as figures weave around the victims. GUARDS *arrange the execution: the slow dance of the technicians. There are the voices; the international films of the mercy throngs; the Death Ritual.*

ETHEL ROSENBERG *and* JULIUS ROSENBERG   We, Julius Rosenberg and Ethel Rosenberg, husband and wife, are now confined in the Death House in Sing Sing Prison, awaiting electrocution on June 18, our fourteenth wedding anniversary. . . .

We appealed to you once before. Our sentence, we declared there, violated truth and the instincts of civilized mankind.

We told you the truth: we are innocent.

The truth does not change. . . .

The guilt in this case, if we die, will be America's. The shame, if we die, will dishonor this generation, and pervade history until future Americans recapture the heritage of truth, justice and equality before the law. . . .

We cannot besmirch our names by bearing false witness to save ourselves. Do not dishonor America, Mr. President, by considering as a condition of our right to survive, the delivery of a confession of guilt of a crime we did not commit. . . .

We submitted proof to show that David Greenglass stole uranium from Los Alamos, in a venture concededly unconnected with us. . . .

We submitted actual physical evidence [the missing console table], never produced in court against us, to show the Greenglasses and the Government collaborated to bring into the trial false testimony that we had in our home an expensive console table, given to us by the "Russians" and equipped for microfilming purposes. It is not a specially constructed table, but one bought by us at R. H. Macy's for about $21 as we testified at our trial. . . .

130

We ask you, Mr. President, the civilized head of a civilized nation, to judge our pleas with reason and humanity.

DWIGHT D. EISENHOWER DEAR SON: To address myself to the Rosenberg case for a minute, I must say that it goes against the grain to avoid interfering in the case where a woman is to receive capital punishment. But in this instance, it is the woman who is the strong and recalcitrant character, the man is the weak one. If there should be any commuting of the woman's sentence without the man's, then from here on the Soviets would simply recruit their spies from among women. I am convinced that the only conclusion to be drawn from the history of this case is that the Rosenbergs have received the benefit of every safeguard which American justice can provide. . . .

JEAN-PAUL SARTRE (*we see the French philosopher speaking to the audience.*) Maintenant que l'on nous a fait vos alliés, le sort des Rosenbergs pourrait être un avant-coureur de notre propre avenir. Vous, qui prétendez être les maîtres du monde, avez eu l'occasion de prouver que vous étiez d'abord maîtres de vous-mêmes. Mais si vous cédez à votre folie criminelle, cette même folie pourrait vous précipiter demain dans une guerre d'extermination. En frappant les Rosenbergs vous avez tout simplement essayé d'arrêter les progrès de la science au moyen d'un sacrifice humain. Par la magie, la chasse aux sorcières, les autodafés, les sacrifices, nous sommes arrivés maintenant au point ou votre pays est malade de frayeur. Vous avez peur de l'ombre de votre propre bombe. Ne soyez pas étonnés si d'un bout à l'autre de l'Europe, nous crions: Attention! l'Amérique est atteinte de la maladie de la Rage! Rompez tout ce qui nous attache à elle, autrement, nous serons à notre tour mordus et enragés!

JEAN-PAUL SARTRE (*simultaneous translation.*) Now that we have been made your allies, the fate of the Rosenbergs could be a preview of our own future. You, who claim to be masters of the world, had the opportunity to prove that you were first

131

masters of yourself. But if you give in to your criminal folly,
this very folly might tomorrow throw us headlong into a war
of extermination. By killing the Rosenbergs you have quite
simply tried to halt the progress of science by human sacrifice.
Magic, witch-hunts, autos-da-fé, sacrifices—we are here getting
to the point: Your country is sick with fear. You are afraid of
the shadow of your own bomb. Do not be astonished if we cry
out from one end of Europe to the other: Watch out! America
has the rabies! Cut all ties which bind us to her, otherwise we
will in turn be bitten and run mad!

In his death costume JULIUS ROSENBERG *steps forward.*

JULIUS ROSENBERG   DEAR MANNY, Never let them change the
truth of our innocence.

For peace, bread and roses in simple dignity we face the
executioner with courage, confidence and perspective—
never losing faith. . . .

P.S. All my personal effects are in three cartons and you can
get them from the Warden. Ethel wants it known that we
are the first victims of American Fascism. All my love—JULIE

*"CASE SEEN IN PERIL," and an eleventh-hour headline and
image chronology begins.*

ETHEL ROSENBERG   DEAREST SWEETHEARTS, my most precious
children, Only this morning it looked like we might be together
again after all. Now that this cannot be, I want so much for
you to know all that I have come to know. Unfortunately,
I may write only a few simple words; the rest your own lives
must teach you, even as mine taught me. At first, of course,
you will grieve bitterly for us, but you will not grieve alone.
That is our consolation and it must eventually be yours. Your
lives must teach you, too, that good cannot really flourish in
the midst of evil; that freedom and all the things that go to
make up a truly satisfying and worthwhile life must
sometimes be purchased very dearly. Be comforted then that

we were serene and understood with the deepest kind of understanding that civilization had not yet progressed to the point where life did not have to be lost for the sake of life, and that we were comforted in the sure knowledge that others would carry on after us. We wish we might have had the tremendous joy and gratification of living our lives out with you. Your Daddy, who is with me in the last momentous hours, sends his heart and all the love that is in it for his dearest boys. Always remember that we were innocent and could not wrong our conscience. We press you close and kiss you with all our strength. Lovingly, DADDY AND MOMMY

STAGE B

MAN IN THE STREET   Are women more concerned with their facial make-up than their all-around appearance?

ANSWER   No comment.

ANSWER   Yes, too many women fail to check their rear appearance.

ANSWER   No, that's what Lady Astor said. . . .

ANSWER   That's true, a woman's first concern is her face. . . .

ANSWER   No comment.

THE DEFENSE   There was a world-wide reaction to their execution. In Paris, thousands participated in rallies to "save the Rosenbergs." One person was shot and over four hundred arrested as demonstrators clashed with massive police formations. In England, supporters made last-minute attempts to persuade Prime Minister Churchill to intervene. In Los Angeles, a strange soap-box orator in Pershing Square convinced two lawyers, that I didn't even know, that I had overlooked something. They went to Justice Douglas and he granted the Rosenbergs, my clients, a stay of execution! The stay was signed and the court adjourned. Then it came over the wire at 6 P.M.: Attorney General Brownell had ordered Chief Justice Vinson to reconvene the court. To reconvene the court—the first time in American history that the court had been asked to convene

133

for the purpose of overthrowing a ruling of one of its own Justices. From all over the country they flew back that night. We went crazy. At the last minute lawyers came into the case from New York. Teams of attorneys went into the homes of judges, they got on their knees; judges were found on golf courses, we pleaded, we begged—they tell me Judge Jerome Frank broke down.

He walks into a new scene.

THE SCREEN *(under the action.)*
U.S. GOVERNMENT BRIEF IN COURT OF AP-
PEALS, 2D CIRCUIT, DOCKET NO. 31259, JUNE
1967.

P. 37 ". . . IT WAS UNEQUIVOCABLY SPELLED
OUT [AT THE TRIAL] THAT THE SKETCH AND
THE GREENGLASS DESCRIPTIVE MATERIAL WAS
NOT OFFERED AS A 'COMPLETE' OR 'DETAILED'
DESCRIPTION [OF THE ATOMIC BOMB], BUT
ONLY AS A 'TIP-OFF.'"

THE DEFENSE   Your Honor, I beg you to order a stay until I can complete my presentation. It would be terrible if I could convince your Honor that you should grant the application and it would be too late.
THE COURT   Get along with your argument: the execution has been moved up to 8 P.M. so as not to conflict with the Sabbath.

THE SCREEN
TELEGRAM

EMANUEL BLOCH
401 BROADWAY NYK

LYONS AND WINCHELL ITEMS FABRICATION
MADE OUT OF WHOLE CLOTH—STOP—NEVER

REFUSED SERVICE OF RABBI—STOP—NEVER
MADE ANY STATEMENTS DIRECTLY OR
INDIRECTLY ABOUT RABBIS THAT SHOWED
ANTI-SEMITISM—STOP—RABBI IRVING
KOSLOWE SING SING CHAPLAIN U.S. MARSHAL
AND AUTHORITIES HERE CAN VERIFY—STOP—
SEE MY LETTERS FEBRUARY 22 AND 23 TO YOU
AND FAMILY DECRYING THESE OUTRAGEOUS
FRAUDS.

JULIUS ROSENBERG 110649

STAGE B

MAN IN THE STREET Do you approve of the verdict in the atom
spy trial?

ANSWER Definitely.

ANSWER Guilty.

ANSWER They're guilty.

ANSWER No comment.

ANSWER No comment.

STAGES A AND B

For the execution there are two DOCTORS, *one* ELECTRICIAN, *three*
PRISONERS. *This group and* THE RABBI, PRISONERS *and* MATRON
*make up the enactment of the electrocution. The entire re-
mainder of the company, however, are present as witnesses.*

A UNITED STATES MARSHAL *stands, obviously waiting for a sign
that* JULIUS ROSENBERG *will talk.* THE MARSHAL *stands with a
telephone in his hand.* JULIUS ROSENBERG *stops and confronts the
outstretched receiver.* THE RABBI *speaks as he walks ahead.*

THE RABBI "Yea, though I walk through the valley of the shadow
of death, I will fear no evil: for Thou art with me . . ."

THE RABBI *continues as* JULIUS ROSENBERG *is strapped in the
chair, the cathode is adjusted, the helmet lowered on the head
to make contact with the shaven spot, the mask is fixed on. The*

first charge dims the lights, shakes the chair, sends up a puff of yellow smoke from the head. The second charge, following a three-second release, lasts for fifty-seven seconds; the third, the same. THE DOCTOR *approaches, rips the shirt open, listens and speaks.*

THE DOCTOR   I pronounce this man dead.

JULIUS ROSENBERG *is placed in a guerney and wheeled out. An* ORDERLY *with a mop and sponge rushes in and cleans the floor and chair. Immediately,* THE RABBI, *leading* ETHEL ROSENBERG, *enters; the* PRISON MATRON *follows.*

THE RABBI
      "In thee, O Lord, do I put my trust;
        let me never be ashamed
      For I have heard the slander of many:
        fear was on every side:
      While they took counsel together against me,
        they devised to take away my life."

Now THE RABBI *sings the Hebrew lament for the dead.*

Smiling softly, ETHEL ROSENBERG *starts toward the electric chair. As she passes the* PRISON MATRON, *she holds out her hand; the older woman grasps it and* ETHEL *draws her close and kisses her lightly on the cheek.*

There are the shocks. THE DOCTOR *advances.*

THE DOCTOR   She is still alive.

The EXECUTIONER *runs out from his cubicle.*

EXECUTIONER   Want another?

There are two more shocks.

THE DOCTOR   I pronounce this woman dead.

ETHEL ROSENBERG *is removed from the stage.*

THE CHORUS

> "So when the Rosenbergs lie dead
> Wrapped in a shroud of Kremlin-red;
> All future traitors should beware
> They too will burn within the 'chair.'"

They pause, then exit repeating the last phrase.

"They too will burn with the 'chair.'"

THE DEFENSE At 7:32 P.M. the White House turned us down for the last time. At 7:45 P.M. Judge Kaufman denied motions for the last time. In New York ten thousand people in Union Square wept and screamed as eight o'clock drew near.

Pause.

Three days later Justice Frankfurter made public his dissenting opinion.

Pause.

It was the way François Mauriac wrote: After years, the long set of appeals and petitions for mercy ended in this violently lighted lacquered room, furnished with a single chair. The man standing on the threshold would have only one word to say, one sign to make, not to cross it. They did not say the word, they did not make the sign. There was only the cruel telephone wire which the day before the Sabbath linked the White House and Sing Sing and which will link them forever.

Pause.

For thirty years I had been an officer of the court. True, I had seen nefarious practices in the criminal courts, but basically I believed in the administration of justice and in the integrity of most officials sworn to uphold it. But how could I dream that officials of the Department of Justice would lend themselves to the perpetration of a complete hoax, like the Jello box business, concocted by these weird characters Gold and the Greenglasses?

137

With emotion.

I was full of fear, too; like the judge and the jury and the man in the street. I suppose that was my biggest mistake, and having those illusions, underestimating the cynicism and power for evil in high places. . . . Maybe that's why I believed to the last minute that they wouldn't dare go through with these executions. I couldn't believe in that much evil. And then not one scientist came forward. I had to accept the Government's word. *They read a list of famous names scheduled as witnesses but they never called them. You have no idea of how lonely it was. Nobody came forward; nobody who knew would come forward to help.*

Pause

"There was truth and there was untruth and if you clung to the truth even against the whole world, you were not mad."

BLOCH *exits.*

THE SCREEN
EMANUEL BLOCH, DIED JANUARY 30, 1954

On the first big screen a giant picture of the real JULIUS ROSEN-BERG *comes up. On the second,* ETHEL ROSENBERG; *and on the third, in the distance, between the parents, the two* ROSENBERG CHILDREN.

There is no curtain call. After a pause there is a dialogue between the audience and the director, actors, and experts on the period.

Afterword

The United States of America v. Julius and Ethel Rosenberg, et al.

Et al.? There were others. Morton Sobell spent a generation as a political prisoner and his wife, Helen, like a creation of Bertolt Brecht, told the story of the outrage up and down the country. There is no room for them in this play. Powerful books by John Wexley and Walter and Miriam Schneir give all the facts that here would have been dramatically unbearable. They are another play: they survived as creative and vital human beings. They lived to see another day. (The actual end of the "age of conspiracy" came, I believe, when Abby Hoffman pole-vaulted into the Brooklyn Navy Yard and announced that he intended to steal the Polaris missile.)

The case went on. The Sobells and their "family" of attorneys pressed the Government for eighteen years. Had the Rosenbergs lived, they would have gone down part of the same long legal road.

1952: Ranking European scientists testified against Greenglass' capacity. Exhibit 8 was still impounded so the Sobell defense was severely handicapped, but the concept of "implosion," the scientists testified, was public knowledge and therefore there was *nothing to steal*. At this time, too, the question of pre-trial publicity was opened. Like almost every other point in the long years of appeal, the matter of State propaganda during political trials, brought to the courts by Morton Sobell and to the public by his wife, has become a seriously contested public issue.

139

1953: The evidence itself was shown to be fatally defective. The console table turned out to be a console table. Prop by prop the Government's case was being shredded.

1956: Mr. Sobell had been kidnapped from Mexico, prior to his arrest, by American agents and not deported as the Government had insisted at the trial. In 1956, after long searching, the attorney Marshall Perlin was able to produce firm evidence of the criminal attack in Mexico.

1966: Morton Sobell, a brilliant engineer, a luminous human being, and a model prisoner, was still denied the parole that anyone else might have expected. Now as his mandatory release date approached, the decision was made to go for the very heart of the case. The Government, fighting to the last, finally lost control of Greenglass' cartoon, Government Exhibit 8. When the shocking sketch that had been the predicate for the great witch-hunts appeared in *The New York Times*, the scandal was complete. At the same moment evidence was brought forward that almost certainly proves FBI forgery in the instance of Harry Gold's New Mexico trip. Suddenly the Government began referring to the fatal Greenglass caricature as "The Strawman"; now the sketch was only "a tip-off," "rhinestones . . . instead of diamonds," no longer was it the "secret of the atom bomb itself!"

There is much more but it is, finally, a question of magic against science: *there was nothing to steal*; no secret formulas *belong* to anyone. The State was defeated, but it persisted nastily; Sobell's pre-trial "jail time" was granted him only after a final judge, ashamed to continue the persecution any longer, ordered it so.

So they, the Sobells, survived. They are public and creative and a growing inspiration (young people immediately sense a kinship with Mr. Sobell, they are drawn to him; he seems to exist in color, like them, while others from the past are in black and white).

To take a step backward from the case is to see a generation of radicals tortured, and beyond them the silent majority—dumb with fear, numb with guilt, irreparably injured by what the State let loose on them—coming into the 1970's astounded by events and broken-hearted at the end of the American Dream

The case is alive because the fears and hopes that underlay the time are still alive. Just as the Government told the Sobells, "If you don't work with us, they'll fry, and you will too," and continued to come to him in prison saying, "The Rosenbergs are dead, you can't help them any more," so the State came to us all and bid us choose, counting on our silence.

It began with the circulation of the transcripts and fact sheets, then meetings, pickets, committees, the poetry and songs and books, and now the plays and films.

The anti-myth is nearing completion. It began when the Rosenbergs and Sobells refused to complete the magic ring which, had they done so, would have reached down to this day and might have led to the actual use of the detention camps. It would not have been a matter of a single or simple "confession" but rather of naming hundreds, thousands, of names; and who could have doubted the word of the atom spy masters themselves?

The beginning of the de-mythologizing process which is rending the country began, in many ways, with their "No!" The "conspiracy" of which they were a real part is just now coming to light: they were the firstlings of the latest and fast-developing American Human Rights Revolution, whose password is always "No!"

141

A Sample of Headlines Shown During the Play

New York Daily News, June 16, 1953
REDS THREATEN 38th PARALLEL
DOUGLAS TO HEAR ROSENBERG PLEA

New York Daily News, June 17
DOUGLAS MUM;
IKE HINTS "NO"

New York Daily News, June 17
GUARD OUR EMBASSIES
IN UPROAR ON A-SPIES

New York Daily News, June 17
POLE FEELS HIS ARMY
WILL TURN ON RUSSIA

New York Daily News, June 17
A-SPIES FACE LAST RULING

New York Daily News, June 18
HOUSE CHEERS MOVE
TO IMPEACH DOUGLAS

New York Daily News, June 19
SPIES GET ONE MORE DAY

New York Daily News, June 19
A-SPIES DEAD-PAN AT NEWS OF DELAY

New York Daily News, June 19
PRISON TENSE A-SPIES CALM

New York Daily News, June 19
ROSENBERG SYMPATHIZERS
IGNORE DEAD SOLDIER

New York Daily News, June 20
SPIES DIE AT SUNSET — EXTRA

New York Daily News, June 20
DOOM—COURT AND IKE
REJECT PLEA OF A-SPIES

New York Daily News, June 20
PAIR ODDLY CONFIDENT;
TOWN ARMED CAMP

New York Daily News, June 20
SPIES DIE IN CHAIR — EXTRA

New York Daily News, June 20
HE GOES TO CHAIR FIRST;
EXTRA SHOCKS FOR HER